LIVING
C*the*ORE
LIFE
from the
INSIDE OUT

"Be the change you wish to see in the world."
—Gandhi

Healthy Living Made Simple

Five secrets to Living a Healthy, Happy, and Empowered Life

DR. AARON GILLESPIE

CONTENTS

Introduction v

Section 1: Living the CORE Life *1*
   Chapter 1:   Our Greatest Problems 7
   Chapter 2:   Aging—Regeneration vs
                 Degeneration 16
   Chapter 3:   CORE Principles 19

Section 2: Steps to Creating a Healthy Lifestyle *29*
   Chapter 4:   Awareness 32
   Chapter 5:   Overcoming the Pain of Change 35
   Chapter 6:   Setting Clearly Defined Goals 42

Section 3: Lifestyle Changes for Living the CORE Life *47*
   Chapter 7:   Diet 49
   Chapter 8:   Exercise 55
   Chapter 9:   Sleep 59
   Chapter 10: Stress 63
   Chapter 11: Emotional and Mental Health 69
   Chapter 12: Relationships and Social Life 72
   Chapter 13: Body Composition 75
   Chapter 14: Your Spine, Posture, and
                 Nervous System 79
   Chapter 15: Using Chiropractic Care for the
                 Health of It 91

***Section 4: Getting Back to Nature and Preparing
our Bodies for a Healthy Life*** *101*
    Chapter 16: How Did Medicine Become
             Mainstream and Nature Become
             the Alternative? 103
    Chapter 17: Seattle to Portland Bike Ride—
             Preparing Your Body for a Healthy Life... 106
Conclusion...................111

INTRODUCTION

Seventeen years ago, my mom called me on the phone, crying, and asked, "Aaron, will you help me? Can I come stay with you for a while?" She had hit rock bottom! My wife and I went to see her, and she looked like a corpse. Her skin was grey. Her face was sunken in—she was wasting away. My dad told me that she had spent most of her days alone, in her room, crying her eyes out. At seventy-two-years old, she was in chronic pain, depressed, anxious, and having panic attacks. She was suicidal and even though she wanted to end her life, she couldn't because her religious beliefs were that suicide is one of the worst sins you could commit. So she stopped eating, having somehow convinced herself that if she didn't eat, she would eventually die and it wouldn't be suicide. Starving yourself to death is a horrible way to go. She was on eighteen different medications, most of which were to counteract the side effects of her other drugs. They had her addicted to methadone for more than a decade. So at seventy-two-years old, she felt like she had no life and no hope for a better future. At this point, she had given up, having already lost decades of her life. Four of the medications had listed side effects that included suicidal thoughts. They weren't even her thoughts. Her thoughts of suicide were chemically induced by the drugs she was taking.

We moved her in with us and started building her a new life, believing she could have a life again without drugs. We started replacing the drugs with a healthier lifestyle that included nutrition, supplementation, exercise, chiropractic adjustments, massage therapy, and hours and hours of talks about her life and how she had gotten here and why she had to change. We knew that her journey ahead was going to be difficult and painful. Until she had hit rock bottom, the pain of change was greater than her perceived benefit of changing—especially when her doctors didn't have any answers for her other than trying another drug. For years, her core belief was that she couldn't survive without the drugs. Do you understand how important your beliefs are? Our beliefs determine our actions and habits, and our actions and habits determine our health and experience of life.

It wasn't long before we had to move her into an assisted living facility to support the intense withdrawal effects of getting off all the drugs she had been on for so many years. It was a long, painful process for her, but she prevailed. I can still remember the first time she told me that she was completely drug free. What a celebration of life that was. She was no longer fighting disease but creating life and health. Before long she was the activities coordinator, the treasurer, the leader of the welcoming committee, and practically running the place. She was talking about getting her driver's license again and even a job. She volunteered at a thrift store several days per week. Eventually, her assisted living facility kicked her out since she no longer needed assisted living. She moved into an apartment with my dad again and started a whole new life. What an exciting time!

Sadly, my mom missed out on much of her life. Before she moved in with us, she lived with my dad in Westport,

Washington, for a year and a half. But because of the drugs she was on, she had no memory of ever living there. At one point, my dad confided in me that for much of my life, she had been on drugs. When I was born, there were complications, and she had a hysterectomy. She not only had pain but also suffered from post-partum depression. Her doctors prescribed her pain killers, muscle relaxants, and anti-depressants. To counteract the side effects of those drugs, she also had been prescribed drugs for constipation, anxiety, sleep, fatigue, etc., etc., etc. The rest is history. She didn't just wake up one day a prescription drug addict. She started taking the first drug, and then gradually over time, it was more and more. Before she knew it, it was out of control and getting worse. Unfortunately, she is not alone since this is what happens to many people.

Though I had been a natural health care provider for fifteen years and I was passionate about helping people live a drug-free life, I couldn't help my mom. It wasn't until she hit rock bottom and finally felt like she had to change, that her mind opened to believe it was possible. After she had gotten off all the drugs and gotten her life back, my dad had a tearful conversation with me and shared how awful he felt about all the times he had taken her from doctor to doctor demanding they find something else to give her. He would have done anything to help her stop the suffering. I believe the doctors were also trying to do their best. They were just doing what they were trained to do: look in their medicine bag for another drug to solve her problem.

But there is another way. There's a reason that more than a million people have died from opioid drugs alone. If you are unhealthy and taking several medications, don't wait until you hit rock bottom to decide to change. Many people find the motivation to change after living through a heart attack or finding out they have cancer. It is attainable for all of us. We must find our own motivation that is strong enough to make sustainable changes that create new habits. Health care should be how we live our lives, not a visit to the doctor.

My dad passed away eight years ago, and my mom will be turning ninety years old in a couple of months. She recently got engaged and acts like a teenager in love. It is awesome to see her enthusiasm and joy for life after so many years of just existing and dreading each day. If she had continued down the road she had been traveling, she would have also missed out on the past two decades.

There is a difference between just biding your time, existing only from one doctor visit to another, and living your life on your terms. If you aren't solid in your principles and don't make conscientious decisions, you may wake up one day and wonder how you got there. Becoming unhealthy is a lifelong journey just like becoming healthy is. Are your doctors or you making your health decisions? You can either choose a lifestyle or a death style. It is important for us all to educate ourselves, develop principles to live by, and make conscientious decisions. Our lives and health are dependent on it!

WHO THIS BOOK IS FOR

This book is for those who want to get more out of their life.

This book is for you if you

- have accepted limitations in your life that you wish you hadn't, and somewhere deep inside, you believe that you can do more, be more, and have more
- feel you are overweight and out of shape; suffer from one or more chronic illnesses; have chronic pain; are stressed out, depressed, or anxious; and are tired of your doctor just prescribing another drug
- are frustrated with where you are in your life, are ready to make a healthy change, and would like to live a long life, filled with health, happiness, and vitality
- are happy with where you are in life and with your health and would like a guide and simple solutions for continuing your healthy life

But if you are looking for a treatment or remedy for some condition or illness, you won't find them here. However, this book might still be your solution. This book comes from the perspective that we are designed to be healthy, and if we have more healthy people, we will have a lot fewer sick people. Most chronic illness comes from people being sick or, in other words, not being healthy.

Living the CORE Life

> *Your body holds deep wisdom.*
> *Trust in it. Learn from it. Nourish it.*
> *Watch your life transform and be healthy.*
> —*Bella Bleue*

The definition of "core" is

1. the tough central part of various fruits, containing the seeds
2. the central or most important part of something

The CORE Life represents the idea of living your life from the inside out and that we have—at our core—the ability to heal. An apple doesn't grow from the outside in, and we don't heal from the outside in. If you get a cut, your skin scabs over to protect the wound, but the actual healing comes from the inside out.

Our core, the most important and central part of us, is life itself. We can't measure it, see it, or quantify it, but we can see and quantify the results of it. Life, or the intelligence that runs our bodies, travels over and through the nervous system, which is at the core of our bodies. Those nerve impulses are constantly transmitted from our brain to our body and from our body to our brain. We live our lives through our nervous system. This is what keeps our body functioning at its best. Life flows from our core. Life flows from the inside out. *The CORE Life* embraces this concept and acknowledges that the intelligence is perfect, so we have the ability to self-regulate and self-heal. We are designed to be healthy.

Our current medical system is very mechanistic. The entire concept is an outside-in approach, which is a big part of why we continue to get sicker and sicker. We don't have a health care system. We have a sick care system, which can be great for saving lives and fighting disease, but it doesn't help us get healthier. It is a big mistake to think that by taking a drug, we will somehow magically be healthier. I am not saying that it doesn't improve our symptoms, but it does take us further from health.

Pharmaceutical companies spend more than six billion dollars per year marketing directly to consumers, and the US spends four hundred billion dollars per year on the drugs.[1] The United States and New Zealand are the only two countries in the world where it is even legal for a pharmaceutical company to market directly to consumers. Is it any wonder that the US consumes significantly more drugs than any other country and more than most combined? Reports indicate that pharmaceutical companies shell out twenty billion dollars per year schmoozing, persuading, and marketing to health

---

[1] Julia Faria, "Pharma and Healthcare Industry Advertising in the U.S.—Statistics & Facts," Statista, updated January 6, 2023, https://www.statista.com/topics/8415/pharma-and-healthcare-industry-advertising-in-the-us.

care professionals to write prescriptions for their drugs.[2] We all know this is a problem, but we are so programmed by it that we have just been sucked in and become numb to it. Americans spent five hundred eleven billion dollars in 2019 on prescription drugs. That was an increase of $200 billion since 2012.

Wow!! Do we really think that science and medicine are solving the riddle of disease? Are you kidding me? If you are just wandering through your life instead of living it on purpose, and then putting all your trust in this system when your health fails you, then it's time for a wake-up call! I encourage you to live *the CORE Life* by putting your trust in your own body's innate, inborn ability to keep you healthy. It is an empowering way to live your life. It is your responsibility to start taking better care of your body. You need to give it more of what it needs and avoid more of what is destructive or toxic to it. You must do this for a lifetime because the human body is adaptable. When you treat it well, it naturally becomes healthier. When you quit taking care of it, it must adapt to the negative environment you are providing for it, so it gets sicker (less healthy). Hopefully, you can see the simplicity of this and its value.

Living *the CORE Life* is a way of creating a healthier body and nervous system that can better self-regulate and self-heal—from the inside out.

Because healthy living has been made so complicated and difficult in the world and the environment we live in, it seems

---

2   Beth Mole, "Big Pharma shells out $20B each year to schmooze docs, $6B on drug ads," Arstechnica, updated January 11, 2019, https://arstechnica.com/science/2019/01/healthcare-industry-spends-30b-on-marketing-most-of-it-goes-to-doctors/.

unattainable for many. It seems overwhelming, and the pain of change seems to outweigh the potential benefits, especially if you believe you are a victim of your health problems and don't believe you have the ability to change them. But healthy living can be simple. I intend to do just that: simplify it. Recognizing your potential and understanding **the CORE Principles** is the answer to change. It is the answer to a better, healthier, happier, and more fulfilling life.

This book will provide five key principles to live by and show you how to apply them in your life, allowing you to simplify healthy living by living a principled life. By developing core principles in your life and living by them, you will not only be physically healthier, but you will also have healthier relationships, healthier financial practices, and healthier, well, everything—in every aspect of your life. This book will empower you to take back your power and take personal responsibility for all aspects of your life. The choices you make give you all the power and control. Once you recognize that the choices you make today will affect the quality of your life in the future, you can begin making better choices and elevate the quality of your life.

You have the choice to

- eat what they tell you to eat, then when you are unhealthy, take what they tell you to take, essentially relying on a sick care system to manage your symptoms and health conditions for the rest of your life and feel like a victim of it

OR

- live *the CORE Life* and simplify healthy living by living **CORE Principles** and accepting responsibility for your life and health

The choice is yours. Choose wisely, my friend!

I wish you the best on your quest for the greatest life you can have. *Go for it. Take action now*! Make it happen.

CHAPTER 1

Our Greatest Problems

"If you can't find what you're seeking, maybe you're looking in the wrong places. Maybe it's been under your nose the whole time, waiting for you."
—*Unknown*

We are looking for answers in the wrong places and we are inundated with information that supports poor lifestyle habits and the need to manage health problems with drugs. After all, most advertising is designed to sell a product and pharmaceutical companies spend billions of dollars pushing an entirely different agenda: to shift an entire health paradigm. They don't even pretend to hide it either. It's in our face every day, and we have become numb. Listen to the drug ads and the horrific side effects. Just the other day I was prescribed an antibiotic for a possible infection under my toenail. When I picked it up at the pharmacy, the pharmacist told me that even though it is rare, some people's skin peels off when using this antibiotic. She assured me that it was rare but that I would know within about thirty minutes. I said, "So, what am I supposed to do if my skin starts to peel off?" She told me to go immediately to the emergency room because it is life-threatening. I told her that I would rather just keep the toe infection and trust my body to heal. Because of our current health paradigm and our belief systems about it, most people don't ask questions or take responsibility for the consequences. They do what they're told and then feel like a victim when things don't go right.

LOOKING IN THE WRONG PLACE

This is our current health paradigm, and we consider this medical system our health care. Yet true health care is how you live your life. Your lifestyle is how you create health. If you have a healthy lifestyle, then you are giving your body all the nutrients it needs and avoiding everything that is toxic to it. From there, we all have an innate inborn intelligence that takes care of the rest. In this model, you can still have medicine as a backup for emergencies, but not as a way of life. What most people don't realize is that when they go to their medical doctor, they are basically saying that they are looking for a pharmaceutical solution for their problem. A lot of people see their medical doctor as a health care provider who will help them find healthy solutions for their problems, and then they get frustrated because their doctors just want to write another prescription. A medical doctor's primary training is in pharmacology, so by going to your medical doctor, you are asking for a pharmaceutical solution for your problem, whether you know it or not. If you had a TMJ problem and went to a dentist, you might get a mouth guard to prevent grinding your teeth. If you went to an acupuncturist for the same TMJ problem, they would use needles. If you went to a massage therapist, they would use massage. If you went to a physical therapist, they would likely give you exercises. If you go to your medical doctor, they may prescribe you anti-inflammatory drugs or something to take for the pain. Since we are all responsible for our own health, it is up to us to decide whether we want to find the most conservative or natural solution or jump right into drugs and surgery. It is unfair to expect your medical doctor to know everything about everything.

Let me give you an example.

Several years ago, my oldest daughter Bri started having severe migraines and a sore, stiff neck. She thought she had overdone it at the gym and wasn't as concerned about her neck as she was about the migraines, so she saw her medical doctor. Her doctor prescribed her high blood pressure medication and Percocet. That was the only answer they had for her. She didn't want to take either of them because she knew they wouldn't do anything to fix the problem, they would only manage the symptoms, and there were significant side effects to the long-term use of these drugs. Isn't that the case with almost all medications prescribed for chronic health conditions? Are any of the medications really designed to correct the problems creating the chronic health problems people suffer from? Have we really gotten to a place where we are just going to be managing our symptoms with drugs for the rest of our lives and call it health care? Bri still resorted to using ibuprofen and, as she tells me now, took more than the recommended dosage every single day. She ended up coming into my chiropractic office, and we found that the problem was really coming from her neck. Through chiropractic adjustments and massage therapy, the migraines subsided. If she only chose to take the drugs she was prescribed, it would have only managed her symptoms and never corrected the problem. I would like to think that this is common sense but unfortunately, the way that people are living their lives don't reflect that. We have way too much chronic illness and disease that is preventable, and we are living on too many medications and continuing to get sicker and sicker.

In essence, we are looking in the wrong place. I remember a time when I couldn't find my keys and knew they were somewhere in my house. I had already looked for hours when somebody finally convinced me to look for them at my office. But because I knew they weren't there, I didn't even want to waste the time looking. Guess where I found them? In my office. I could have spent an eternity looking in my house, but I never would have found them. If you are trying to find the key to why we are so unhealthy and why we keep getting sicker, studying and spending billions of dollars on genetics and drugs will never get you the answer. An eternity of time and all the money in the world spent fighting disease will never bring us the answer to creating a healthier world. We will never, ever, create a healthier human race by fighting disease. The greatest defense against disease is to be healthy. I'm not saying scientists and doctors should stop fighting disease, but what if we spent even a tenth of the money on creating healthier people? We would have a lot fewer diseases to fight.

RIV—OUR CURRENT SYSTEM IS TEACHING THE WRONG MESSAGE

When Riv, my middle child, was fourteen years old, their blood sugar spiked to 862 and they were diagnosed with type 1 diabetes. Because this is such a serious condition and potentially life-threatening, the doctors were very proactive at getting them on insulin and starting them on an educational program so Riv could understand the condition and how to manage it. At the first educational meeting, the instructor started by assuring them that it wasn't their fault. They emphasized over and over that it had nothing to do with anything that Riv had ever done. It was not related to their diet or exercise and was not a result of any lifestyle or environmental factors. The instructor went on to assure them that they could continue to have as much cake, ice cream, pizza, and donuts as they want. All they needed to do is increase the amount of insulin they take. Every food choice the instructor mentioned was a very unhealthy choice. None of them could even be considered real food. Essentially, they wanted to make sure that Riv completely felt like a victim of this disease and that they would just have to spend the rest of their life managing it. I understood what they were trying to do. While I had hoped they wouldn't take this same approach if it was type 2 diabetes, many with type 2 have told me they are getting the same message. They could have done a much better job teaching Riv and all patients with any type of diabetes to make better choices and taken this opportunity to empower them by sharing what they do have control over and that their choices and habits will have an impact on how this disease affects them and the rest of their life. I was so disappointed in the system!

I started to study diabetes and realized just how huge this problem is. I read that one in ten adult Americans has been diagnosed with it and that one in four is over sixty-five years of age, not to mention all those that are pre-diabetic and have not been diagnosed yet. Those numbers are growing and show no sign of slowing down. That is a massive problem! I also learned that 90–95 percent of those cases are type 2 diabetes. At least with type 2 diabetes, most of the leading experts agree that it is preventable and reversible. (By the way, this is true of most of the other chronic health conditions listed earlier in this book. With diabetes, though, the consequences can be horrific. People die from this condition. They have heart disease, kidney failure, blindness, and even amputated limbs.) This made me really wonder if everyone knows these problems are preventable, why do so many people have them? It's not because people don't know that if they ate better and exercised more, they would be healthier. It's not because people don't know that if they replaced their drugs with a healthier lifestyle, they would feel better and have more energy. I think I know why.

People are living in fear and feel like a victim, so they ignore the potential consequences. They feel apathetic that their choices will have a significant impact on their health. This, in turn, leads to them feeling dependent on their doctors and drugs to manage their health problems and willing to live with the consequences as if they have no other choice. We all have choices, and our choices make a difference.

Your body is designed to be healthy. If you create a healthy body, it won't have high blood pressure. It won't have high cholesterol or high blood sugar. It won't have osteoporosis. It won't have digestive problems. When you improve your health, chronic health problems get better. They might not be perfect, but they get better.

WHO SHOULD WE TRUST WITH OUR HEALTH?

I get it. We all want to trust the FDA, the CDC, the AMA, and Big Pharma. Since Big Pharma has more money than the rest combined, I guess it is also likely that they control the rest. A lot of people think that anyone that questions any of them must be a conspiracy theorist. Let's have a reality check. I don't think anyone knows the truth or depth of the corruption of any of these organizations. If you think that none of it exists and you can totally trust them all, maybe you are right. You can choose to believe that they are all perfectly honest and only looking out for our best interests and don't take profits, personal gain, or power into account. You can probably find information to support your beliefs on either side. Since nobody really knows, you can choose to believe what you want. You are responsible for your health so make sure you take time for a reality check.

If you choose to believe this and you follow along with everything you are told and you are wrong, you can't blame anyone but yourself. Most people don't want to take responsibility, so they won't even do their own research. It is easier to blame the doctors, the system, or the drugs. But either way, it doesn't change the outcome. We are clearly not a healthy society.

Let's take a look at some research and you can decide who to trust. Let's take the American Heart Association since I used to hold them in the highest regard. They are one of the most popular charity/non-profit organizations in America and fund cardiovascular research and educate consumers on healthy living. Did you ever ask yourself how Cocoa Puffs, Frosted Flakes, Lucky Charms, Trix, and French Toast Crunch got their endorsement from the American Heart Association that they are heart-healthy products? Money! The American Heart Association is partially funded by making endorsements. Apparently, for the right price, you can get your product endorsed as being heart healthy. And this is who we are trusting to teach us healthy living. OK, so they have removed those endorsements and made the requirements stricter after getting called out on it, but should we really have to worry so much about who to trust? General Mills can say that the cereal contains thirteen essential vitamins and minerals and extra fiber, and the AHA endorses them, and somehow people buy in, hook, line, and sinker. Are you really buying this? If you want to eat the cereal, go ahead. It is your choice, but you shouldn't do it because you believe that it is heart healthy.

If you tend to be trusting of the pharmaceutical industry, all you need to do is do a Google search. All the information is readily available to the public. In 2012, GlaxoSmithKline paid out $3 billion in a settlement for criminal penalties for off-label promotion and failure to disclose safety data. Between 2009 and 2013, Pfizer, Johnson and Johnson, Abbott Laboratories, and Eli Lilly paid out an additional $5.1 billion in in criminal offenses for off-label promotion and kickbacks, false claims, and failure to disclose safety data. In 2008, Merck paid out almost a billion dollars for civil and criminal penalties for Medicare fraud, false claims as to cardiovascular safety, and kickbacks. According to a report from CNBC, Merck settled Vioxx claims for $4.85 billion for heart attacks and strokes that thousands of users suffered from. The reason they received criminal fines was that they made false claims about cardiovascular safety so they could sell it for billions of dollars. Vioxx was approved by the FDA in 1999, and it was estimated by the *Lancet* that 88,000 Americans had heart attacks from taking Vioxx, and 38,000 of them died. They still pocketed billions of dollars from the sale of Vioxx, even after paying out all the fines and penalties. In a report from the Department of Justice in 2012, they state that the judge imposed nearly $322 million in fines for illegal activities from Merck for providing false statements about the drug's cardiovascular safety. Merck made more than $10 billion selling Vioxx, not to mention how much their stock prices increased, and was required to pay out only $322 million by the Justice Department. No one went to jail, and 38,000 people died from a drug that they knew caused cardiovascular problems. I could go on and on, but you get the idea. It is difficult to find a pharmaceutical company that hasn't been found guilty of civil and criminal offenses.

When drug companies push a drug to market, they automatically build into the pricing the cost of paying out fines, penalties, and lawsuits. If you can make $10 billion off a drug and only have to pay $2 billion in fines, lawsuits, and penalties, then you still have a nice profit. It's the world we live in. Why do you think you are unable to sue a pharmaceutical company for vaccine injury? The pharmaceutical industry got together and told the government that they would no longer produce vaccines if they could be sued for their harm. It's just too costly because they all have potentially risky side effects and when introduced to an entire population, they just couldn't survive the litigation. We want to pretend it doesn't exist and they are looking out for our best interest; however, it is important to make your health care decisions with your eyes fully open. If we can all do that, then we will no longer need to make excuses or feel like a victim anymore. There is definitely a time and place for medicine, but it has become severely abused. Somewhere along the line medicine became mainstream and nature became the alternative. Should we trust medicine or the intelligence that took a sperm and an egg and animated human life?

CHAPTER 2

Aging—Regeneration vs Degeneration

"There are two ways to live your life. One is as though nothing is a miracle. The other is as though everything is a miracle."
—*Albert Einstein*

When you improve your health, you also improve your chances of aging gracefully. One of the problems with our health system is we view old age as an automatic excuse for poor health. Yes, our bodies do degenerate with age because every cell in our body has a life span. When it dies, it is replaced by a new cell. This is one cycle of regeneration. Every type of tissue has a different life span determined by your individual plan stored in your DNA. Each individual person has a different plan than the next. The plan is stored in the DNA but controlled, regulated, and carried out by innate intelligence (life) by transmitting information over the nervous system. When we are young, with each cycle of regeneration, the cells get stronger and healthier. We are adapting and evolving. As we get older, with each cycle of regeneration, the cells get weaker and less adaptable (less healthy). So, yes, there is a natural process of aging. But—and this is important to note—the speed of aging has everything to do with how healthy our cells, organs, and tissues are. Unhealthy or damaged cells will degenerate or age faster while healthy cells will age slower—meaning the speed of aging has less to do with time and more to do with the health of our bodies and nervous systems. When someone injures a joint, for example, it heals with scar tissue. This tissue is not the same as it once was. If not rehabilitated properly, through the healing process, then it won't function properly. This abnormal function leads to degeneration or an accelerated aging process where each cycle of regeneration is weaker and less healthy than the last. The unfortunate thing is that the worse it gets, the faster it gets worse. For example, a person could have degeneration in their spine and their doctor may tell them it is normal for their age. Yet, if you look two spinal segments away, those bones will look young, strong, and healthy. If you have some bones that are degenerated and some that are healthy, which ones do you think are normal for your age? What your doctor is really telling you is that it is common for your age. In other words, many people your age also have degeneration. What they, often times, aren't telling you is that it is preventable. When you practice in a sick care model and study how to fix the body with drugs or surgery, they are right. In this model, there are no solutions because you can't use a sick care system to solve a health care issue.

But it is preventable. There is a solution: create a healthier body and you will slow down the aging process. We have more control over our aging than we give ourselves credit for. This is the empowering part. We all have choices for what we believe. Our choice might be influenced by our doctors, teachers, commercials, family beliefs, and how we were raised, but in the end, we all have a choice in what we believe. You can believe that you are a victim of your circumstances and genetics, or you can choose to believe that your choices (lifestyle) influence your health, your quality of life, your aging process, your happiness, and your vitality. The choice is yours. Your life depends on it.

If you believe that you are responsible for your life and health and want to take back your power, then follow me on the journey of living *the CORE Life*, which is based on five principles. You will learn about these principles in the next chapter.

CHAPTER 3

CORE Principles

"A man without principles is as a ship without a rudder—at the mercy of every wind and wave."
—Christopher Charles

M y mission is to empower as many people as possible to make changes in their life for the better. *The CORE Life* is intended to make healthy living simple, to reduce the pain of change, and to empower you to believe that there is a better you in your future. Living *the CORE Life* is not about how we can get by and just survive. It's about how we can be the best version of ourselves. It is an honest look at what we can do to create the healthiest body we can. None of us will ever achieve perfection in living a healthy life but taking responsibility for our life and health is the first step and necessary to really feel empowered.

To live *the CORE Life*, here are five important principles to live by.

CORE PRINCIPLE #1

> The human body is self-healing, self-regulating, and self-maintaining, and there is an inborn, innate intelligence that runs, regulates, coordinates, and regenerates every organ and system of the body.

This is the foundational, fundamental principle of *the CORE Life*. If at any point in this book, you feel like making excuses for where you are in your life or feel like you are a victim of your circumstances, genetics, or anything else for that matter, look back to this principle. It is the answer to change. It is the answer to a healthier, happier life.

The center of control for the intelligence discussed in this principle is the brain. Signals are transmitted over and through the nervous system to control and regulate the entire human body. In essence, life flows through your nervous system to organize and coordinate matter into a living being. The English language doesn't have a word to define what takes the information contained in our DNA and applies the force necessary to make all the cells, organs, and systems of the body work with perfection and adapt properly in every situation to allow us to live and thrive. We just take that intelligence for granted. It is life itself that makes that happen. If you were asked, "What makes your eyes water when you get dirt in them?" you might say that it was the dirt that caused your eyes to water or maybe even say it's your tear ducts that do it. But a dead person has tear ducts, yet they don't water. So, what is it that causes your tear ducts to excrete tears to flush out the dirt? We know that you must be alive for that to happen, but does anyone really say, "It is life that causes your eyes to tear up"?

What really happens is that when the dirt hits your eye, sensory nerves send signals from your eye to your brain, telling it that something is in your eye. Your brain then sends a signal back to the tear ducts and tells them to secrete tears to protect your eye. It doesn't tell your pancreas to produce insulin. It doesn't tell your pituitary gland to secrete growth hormone. It tells your tear ducts to produce tears. That is Intelligence—Innate (inborn) Intelligence. It is the expression of life itself, through the nervous system. We live our lives through our nervous systems. Your entire body must be perfectly regulated to stay alive. We take this for granted. Things like heart rate, blood pressure, body temperature, body fluid levels, blood sugar levels, etc., can only have small fluctuations for us to stay alive but even smaller fluctuations for us to stay healthy. An innate intelligence keeps it all in check and working perfectly, yet when it comes to health issues, this intelligence, and the way it communicates with the body, gets ignored and only the organ itself is looked at to find the problem. Apparently, we can only have hardware problems. Without a word to define this energy, intelligence, or life force, it is just an abstract concept, and so it gets ignored. For the purpose of this book, we will refer to it as innate intelligence or just simply Innate.

CORE PRINCIPLE #2

You are responsible for your life and health.

We are all different and have different potential, so we can't compare ourselves to anyone else. Most of us know someone who can seemingly eat whatever they want and as much as they want yet are still as skinny as a rail. I've heard people say in a jealous rant, "I hate you. If I just look at a french fry, I put on two pounds." If you are always comparing yourself to other people, you will likely find yourself disappointed and give up.

In order to feel empowered, we must

- only compare who and what we are today to who and what we dream to become
- decide that we want the best version of ourselves
- decide that we want to improve

It is a choice, but you must decide. Perfection is unattainable, but improvement is possible for every one of us. That's all it takes. So, it is up to each one of us to change and improve. It doesn't happen by accident. You must believe and have faith that there is a better life out there for you and then decide to change.

If you can accept the idea that your life and health currently are the result of everything that you have done over your lifetime, then you should realize that if you had done things differently, you would have had a different outcome. If you had become a drug addict or chosen a life of crime, you know things would be different. If you chose a different job, career, spouse, town, etc., it would have led to a different outcome. So too if you had eaten differently, exercised more or less, or had different sleeping habits, your current health would be different. The same is true about your future.

We are creatures of habit, and it is our habits that created who we are today. So only a change in your beliefs and habits will create a better you. Too many people wander through life reacting to circumstances and feeling like a victim when things don't turn out the way they want. This is like someone on a sailboat not using their sails. They could sit there all day, look in the direction they want to go, visualize it and wish for it, and even set a goal to go in that direction, but until they take action and set their sails, they will feel like a victim of the wind and currents. Taking positive action consistently creates habits and rituals, and that is what creates change.

So, decide what you want, make a plan, and then take action! If you accept this principle to be true, then the choice to not make a plan is also a choice, and you must accept the responsibility for the consequences of your actions or lack of actions. Where we are in our life is directly related to all the choices we have made along the way. This is not only true for our health, but also for our jobs/careers, relationships, finances, where we live, and most everything else. This is a good time for an honest look in the mirror. Our choices affect everything! Make good choices!

CORE PRINCIPLE #3

> If you give your body more of what it needs and avoid more of the things that are toxic to it, you will become healthier.

This principle is why it is simpler than most people think. They don't realize how even small changes in their lifestyle can make significant changes to their health. They procrastinate because it feels like a daunting task to change their diet or start an exercise program or change their sleeping habits. Procrastination is the thief of health! Another problem is that too often people compare themselves to others.

Your actions today will affect the outcome in your future. This is the part we have the most control over. We no longer have control over the past. So, you don't have to feel guilty about having made poor choices in the past. Instead, accept responsibility. There is a big difference psychologically. Accepting responsibility is empowering, while taking the blame just leaves us feeling guilty. When you feel empowered, you are more likely to take action. Remember, the more good things you do and the fewer bad things you do will lead to a better outcome. We can sit back and complain about what is wrong or make better choices to affect our future.

The problem is that we were never given the owner's manual for the human body. We don't know for sure how to maximize our human potential. That is why it is so important to live your life based on principles. What we do know is that the body has needs. For the purpose of this book, we will call those needs nutrients. Nutrients are those things the body needs in order to function optimally. It isn't just food and water. For example, we will be calling sleep a nutrient. We will be calling air a nutrient. We will be calling love and human connection nutrients. We will be calling exercise a nutrient. These are a few of our basic needs; however, the quality and quantity of each of these will affect the ability of the body to function and adapt optimally (health). This is also the part of our life that we have control over. We call this lifestyle. This is also the part of our life that most people make excuses for. We don't know exactly what the perfect diet is, exactly how much sleep we need, or how much exercise we need and what types are ideal for each person. Even the experts disagree. Some of the things that we believed to be true twenty years ago, we now know were false. All we can do is make the best choices based on what we do know. I believe that each of us would probably have a little different recipe based on our genetics, our body types, and our performance needs. We are not striving for perfection. Remember, we are striving for personal improvement.

To do that, you need to know what the nutrients and toxins are. Some toxins like fast food are obvious, but some are less obvious. Every prescription drug *is* toxic, and even though some may seem necessary, it is important to acknowledge that they are all *toxic* to the human body and its potential to function optimally. In fact, the sole intention of prescription drugs is to override how the body is functioning. There are side effects to every drug and a laundry list for most. The reason for this is that they are interfering with the body's natural functions. Remember, to improve health, we must increase nutrients and decrease toxins.

Fear and negativity are toxins that are just as bad as fast food and a sedentary lifestyle. While we know what fast food and a sedentary lifestyle do to our body, we may think that fear and negativity have no impact on our health, but they do. They have been found to increase stress hormones. On a chronic basis, this keeps your body in a sympathetic dominant (fight or flight) state, preventing your body from functioning in an optimal state. It reduces your ability to adapt, and since we already agreed that health equals adaptation, you absolutely need to reduce fear and negativity and replace them with hope, positivity, and empowerment to optimize your genetic health potential.

You may use the excuse that you don't know what the "good" choices are, but I think we are clear about some of the human body's basic needs. Most everyone could drink more water, exercise more, eat more nutritious food, sleep better, meditate or do more yoga, have better relationships, love more, give more, have more gratitude, be more positive, stress less, consume less toxic food and medications, and expose themselves to less negativity. I think you get the idea. The healthier we are, the less sick we get. You may feel like you are the victim of some chronic condition—or, like most Americans, many chronic conditions—and it is just your lot in life. But what if you just considered that if you were healthier, based on better choices, you may not have some of these conditions? Right or wrong, I think the principle is sound and worth considering. Can we just agree that the more good we do, and the less bad we do, the better the outcome?

CORE PRINCIPLE #4

Health and healing take time and are a continuous process.

Health and healing are not a destination but a constant journey. You must build a lifestyle that is based on healthy choices, or you will always be at the mercy of fighting chronic illness and disease. The quality of our health is directly related to the quality of our lifestyle. Someone could eat a good diet for ninety days, or a year, or five years, but if they stop eating nutritious food and exercising, live with chronic stress, have bad sleeping habits, etc., it doesn't take long and their health declines rapidly. The human body has nutrients that are necessary, not only for survival but also for being healthy. So, you always need those nutrients, not just sometimes. People can start a new diet or exercise plan and lose a bunch of weight and start feeling great. But when they go back to their previous lifestyle, they end up right back where they started. Poor health habits lead to poor health. Great health habits lead to great health! It's that simple!

CORE PRINCIPLE #5

The human body is adaptable.

Health can be defined as the ability of the body to adapt to its environment. Being healthy doesn't mean you will never get sick or injured. It means that your body quickly adapts to the injury, bacteria, or virus and heals. If we could quantify health, it would be the ability of the human body to adapt to its internal and external environment. This takes us back to principle #1. The human body has an **innate intelligence** that allows it the ability to adapt. Many experts in science and medicine give credit to hormones for regulating all the systems of the body. It always shocks me that as intelligent as many of them are, they don't even address the fact that all the hormones are being regulated. What is it that regulates which hormones are produced, in what quantities, and where they are sent? You see, science can measure and quantify the hormones, but it can't measure and quantify the innate intelligence that regulates them. Let's give credit where credit is due.

If you are out in the heat and your body temperature rises, hormones are released (regulated by **Innate**) to cause you to sweat. If you were out in the desert without water, you would initially sweat to bring down your rising body temperature. You wouldn't sweat forever, though. Eventually, you would start to become dehydrated and other hormones would be released (also regulated by **Innate**) to stop you from sweating. The hormones can only do their individual jobs. If your body temperature gets too high, it can kill you. If your body fluid levels get too low, it can kill you. Who do you want to make the decisions for you about how much you sweat and when you need to retain water? A scientist, a doctor, or the innate intelligence that took a sperm and egg cell and created this amazing human being you are today and has kept you alive your whole life? Not trusting the ability of the body to adapt properly to its environment has caused us to make horribly destructive health decisions. This brings us to our greatest problems.

SECTION 2
Steps to Creating a Healthy Lifestyle

"The groundwork of all happiness is good health."
—Leigh Hunt

Awareness. Take an honest look at where you are and how you got there. Accept responsibility for creating the person you are today. Don't make excuses for anything. If you do, you can't change it. With this attitude and belief, you have the greatest likelihood of making positive change.

Attitude and belief. It all starts with attitude. Believe it or not, you have almost complete control over your attitude. Attitude and beliefs go hand in hand. However, in order to change your beliefs, you must decide that your current beliefs aren't serving you and decide that you want to change them. Deciding to change your attitude will cause you to read different books, watch different videos, and hang around different people. With that said, I do recognize that it is hard to change our beliefs that we have developed over a lifetime. We have learned these beliefs from our childhood upbringing, our teachers, our doctors, and too much from TV, media, and commercials. They tend to be constantly reinforced by our friends and family members. So, if you want to change your beliefs to a more empowering set of beliefs and make your health a stronger core value, you may need to spend more time with people that support this new empowering belief system. Read books and watch videos that support this belief system. I believe that if you want to live a healthy life, you must make health your passion, your hobby. You must find a way to make it fun for you.

Develop your why. You should be consistently looking at why it is important to be healthy. The stronger and more emotional this reason is for you, the more likely your success. This needs to be an ongoing process just like eating a good diet or getting regular exercise. Otherwise, when you look or feel better, your why shrinks and you will fall back into unhealthy habits.

Set goals. For years I dreamed of being a professional speaker. I had put it on my vision board and dreamed that one day I would be on the big stage just like some of my favorite speakers that I had watched and listened to for years. I was in Toastmasters, took professional speaking courses, and spoke locally at businesses and organizations, however, I didn't do any of the things necessary to take it to the next level. What was holding me back? It was always a little frustrating for me because as much as I dreamed and wished for it, I wasn't really doing anything to make it happen. One year I went to a Tony Robbins seminar and one of his messages changed everything for me and has stuck with me to this day. He said that you must have goals that are consistent with the work you are willing to do, or you will be constantly frustrated and set yourself up for failure. I realized that when I looked at the people that were traveling the world speaking and moving the masses, I wasn't willing to walk in their shoes. I wanted to be an influencer, have their following, and make the impact they were making, but I wasn't willing to make the sacrifices they made. So, as you set your goals, make sure they are consistent with the work you're willing to do or the life you are willing to have. With that realization, I was able to release that goal. I felt like a weight was lifted. In terms of health goals, sometimes people look at someone else and wish they could have their body, but if they could pull back the curtains, they wouldn't be willing to walk in their footsteps. So, make sure that when you set your end goal, you are willing to do what it takes to make it happen or you will be setting yourself up for failure. When setting your health goals, strive for improvement, not perfection.

Commit and take action. After setting your goal, commit to doing it. If your commitment is for too long, it sets you up for failure.

OK! It's the moment of truth! What are you going to do? If you continue to do exactly what you have been doing, you will get more of what you have, only it gets worse. If you do more good and less bad, you get healthier, guaranteed! It's that simple! It's a universal law! It's a *CORE Principle*! The degree that your health improves is directly proportional to how much change you make to your current lifestyle.

Now let's investigate these steps in more detail and see how they can help you create a healthier lifestyle.

CHAPTER 4

Awareness

*"Your visions will become clear only when
you can look into your own heart. Who looks
outside, dreams, who looks inside, awakes."*
—C.G. Jung

I was originally going to title this chapter "acceptance" because in order to change, you must accept where you are. But I think that is a big part of our problem: too many people just accept where they are in their life, as if they are the victim of it. It even sounds apathetic. Awareness is much better. An honest look in the mirror is the first step in making change.

Let's first look at our picture globally. Chronic illnesses and diseases have reached epidemic proportions today. We have had more heart disease, cancer, diabetes, obesity, allergies, asthma, skin problems, infertility, sleeping problems, digestive problems, anxiety, and depression, etc., etc. than ever in history, and they all continue to get worse. We are not curing cancer or any of these other problems by developing a new drug or a new vaccine. We just keep getting sicker. Have you noticed? The answers will never be found by studying genetics. People are so quick to say, "It runs in my family."

What has changed more dramatically in the last hundred or thousand years or even the last twenty years for that matter, our genes or the environment? I think we can all agree that our environment has changed the most.

The only real solution to this global epidemic is to become healthier and stronger by improving our lifestyle. Our choices make a difference. Most of us know that the junk we eat and our stressful, inactive lifestyles lead to being weak and unhealthy, but then we expect the doctors to find out what is wrong with us and fix us with their drugs. If you step back and look at the big picture, you can see that our problem is in our health paradigm. The problem lies in our belief system. And it is a huge problem. If you don't believe me, just look at what is being sold most in grocery stores. Look at what is in the grocery carts. Look at the amount of soda and energy drinks sold every day. Look at the lines of people in the drive-thru at fast-food restaurants. Then look at all the people filling the urgent care centers, standing in lines at pharmacies, and waiting in emergency rooms for help with a chronic illness and disease. We are not in great shape. Even when I'm at the gym, it is almost rare to see people in their fifties that are in great shape, let alone forties or even thirties. Even the kids are overweight today. It isn't our genes; it's our environment and how we choose to live our lives.

89 percent of adults aged sixty-five or older are taking one or more prescription drugs, and more than half, 54 percent, are taking four or more.[3] It doesn't just affect seniors, as 25 percent of American kids are on at least one prescription drug

[3]   Ashley Kirzinger, "Data Note: Prescription Drugs and Older Adults," Health Reform, KFF, August 9, 2019, https://www.kff.org/health-reform/issue-brief/data-note-prescription-drugs-and-older-adults/.

for chronic illnesses. Kids are the leading growth sector of the pharmaceutical industry, and at the current growth rate, up to 50 percent of American kids could be on prescription drugs by the year 2050. This is a problem. It is a massive problem! The saddest part is that the leading experts consider most of these conditions preventable. I know that we look to medicine for our solutions, but I hope that you can at least consider the possibility that medicine is also a huge part of our problem.

Philosophically, the approach is that the problem is outside of you and the solution should also come from the outside. It puts us in the position of feeling like the victim. "It's not my fault." It's easier that way. None of us really want to take the blame for our problems. And I don't want you to take the blame or feel guilty either, but I do want you to take responsibility. There is a big difference between accepting responsibility and taking the blame or feeling guilt. Remember, *CORE Principle #2: You are responsible for your life and health*. This leads us to empowerment. Once you have awareness and accept responsibility, you are well on your way to making change. Change is never easy, though.

CHAPTER 5

Overcoming the Pain of Change

"Change happens when the pain of staying the same is greater than the pain of change."
—*Tony Robbins*

You can agree that all that is left to do is change. But change is not always easy. Change can be painful. When I was just out of high school, I started chewing tobacco. I ended up chewing for about twelve years. It wasn't that it was always a pleasurable experience. In fact, my gums had receded to where the roots of my teeth were exposed, and they would get so inflamed, bloody, and painful that I couldn't chew in that spot. I would move the chew to the back and to the upper lip until sometimes my whole mouth was raw. It doesn't sound all that intelligent now, but that's how strong addiction is. Throughout my twenties, I had lots of friends show me pictures of lip cancer, gum cancer, and tongue cancer. The pictures were gruesome! I knew the consequences but chewed anyway. I always thought that I would quit one day—and certainly before it got that bad. But since I didn't feel any sense of urgency, I continued to chew. I didn't believe there would be consequences tomorrow, so I procrastinated.

I am so thankful now that I finally reached a point where my why got strong enough to change. Making lifestyle changes isn't easy. Many people out there desperately need to change, but they aren't ready or willing to change yet. But many more desire to have a better, happier, healthier, and more fulfilling life. Hopefully, that is you. If it is, *the CORE Life* is for you.

POWER OF BELIEFS

It all starts with your beliefs. If you don't believe you control your life and are not a victim, then you will always find excuses that are stronger than your why. Your faith and belief in human potential must be strong to overcome the constant programming we are all getting every day from the pharmaceutical industry. They are spending billions of dollars on marketing, not just to sell their products but to influence a belief system that makes us dependent on them, and our health care providers are teaching this. It is constant fear motivation. I can't tell you how many of my patients with high blood pressure have said their doctor has it under control with medication. They aren't exercising any more or eating any better. They are just managing it with meds. Are they being told that they can heal themselves by changing their lifestyle? Are they being told the consequences of not changing? Do they just not care? Are they too apathetic?

Wouldn't we all be healthier if we gave our body more of what it needs and avoided more of what is harmful to it? There it is. That's it. That's all there is to it! It is that simple! If you couldn't see the potential before, then hopefully you can now. Do more good, and less bad. Believe in your potential and the power you have to affect your life and health with the choices you make, and you will be able to change.

ATTITUDE AND PERCEPTION

Most people don't realize that they have control over their attitude. They think pessimism and negativity are genetic traits. Nope! It's a choice! Could you imagine if people said that if they ate a good diet and exercise regularly, they wouldn't be being true to themselves? You can choose to believe that your attitude is a genetic trait, or you can choose to believe that your attitude is a choice. Either way, it's a choice!

Your beliefs are a choice! Your attitude is a choice! Remember *CORE Principle #2:* **You are responsible for your life and health.**

If you choose to believe that it is just genetics, you could spend your life living out of a pill bottle in an assisted living center, existing through the last decades of your life, instead of living the life you dream you could have.

Some people say that they are just being realistic. People tend to think that reality is whatever their perception is. No! It is just their perception. What if you could change your perception? You can! People make *excuses* for their negative attitude because they are reacting to their circumstances. Nobody wants to feel like a failure. If you choose to believe that you are a victim of your circumstances or genetics or anything else, then you are right and you didn't fail because it was outside of your control. That's the easy way out. Of course, things that happen to us, or things that are genetic, can limit our potential. But you have control over what you do with your circumstances or genetics, or whatever else you feel a victim of. You can wallow in your pity party, or you can pull up your britches and choose to make the best out of your life. Positive people don't necessarily have the most positive circumstances in their life; they just choose to be positive. They choose a different perception of their circumstances. If you change your perception, it will change your perspective.

If you investigate the lifestyle of a pessimistic, negative person, you may find that they don't like their jobs and work with people that are negative and complain a lot. They may hang around with people or have family members and friends that are negative and gossip and love to watch the news or CNN (**C**onstantly **N**egative **N**ews). The most negative people I know do not feel like they have or serve a purpose in this life greater than themselves. Purpose, hope, empowerment, and love are nutrients and important to optimize our human potential! A negative attitude is a toxin; a positive attitude is a nutrient. So, if you increase your positivity, your body will function at a higher level.

Once you have changed your perspective and made the choice to be more positive, you can set well-defined, clear goals that help to create and reinforce the attitudes, perceptions, and perspectives you wish to live your life by. This is how you live an empowered life on your terms and not feel like a victim. You could set a goal to not watch the news for thirty days, to read a chapter of a positive or inspirational book every day, to read positive affirmations every day, or to limit time with the negative people in your life.

HOW TO CHANGE

Change, however, is hard even when the principle behind the change is simple.

Step 1 Believe. As we have established, the first step is to believe that if you change your habits or, what we call our lifestyle, you have the potential to have better health and to heal yourself.

Step 2 Find your why. Figure out what your strongest motivator is and write it on a 3 X 5 index card and read it every morning. If you are really committed to change, make several of them. Put one on your bedside table and read it every morning when you wake up. Put one in your car and read it on the way to work. Put one at work and read it when you get there. Put one on your refrigerator and pantry door and read them when you open the doors. When you are constantly reminding yourself of why it's important for you to live healthy habits, you are more likely to succeed.

Some people want to lose weight so they look good, while others just don't want to have a heart attack and die. Some want the joy of being able to play with their grandkids or want an active lifestyle as they age. Some fear being debilitated in a nursing home. Some are sick and tired of having allergies, asthma, or digestive problems, or being chronically fatigued. But too many people just give up and accept their limitations. They lose faith in their potential. What motivates you? What is your why? You must have a strong why to overcome the pain of change. Finding a why that is stronger than the pain of change will motivate you to decide to change! Unfortunately, motivation is generally not enough to sustain change, but commitment is.

Step 3 Make goals. I go into detail on this step in the next chapter.

Step 4 Commit and take action. Motivation can help you decide to change, while commitment will sustain the change long enough to create new habits. If it is a short-term commitment, then you need to consistently recommit.

On January 1st of this year, I decided to commit to working out every day for the month of January. I was already exercising three–five times per week, so it didn't seem like a huge stretch. I found that it wasn't nearly as easy as I thought. Some days I had planned to work out at lunch, but things happened that made it impossible. Most of the time, I would just go right after work instead, but there were times we had dinner plans right after work. I would try to get out of work a little early so I could get in a short workout before dinner, even if I had to be a little late to dinner. When I couldn't get out of work early, I knew I would have to either go to dinner late or work out after dinner. Once we had a couple of martinis and didn't leave the restaurant until about 9:30 p.m., the last thing I felt like doing was going to the gym to work out. But I went. If I hadn't gone, it wouldn't have been from a lack of motivation, it would have been from a lack of commitment. Some people say they are committed but use the excuse they didn't have time. Truth is, that shows a lack of commitment.

My commitment was strong enough to make it through thirty days, but my commitment would not have been strong enough to make it for a year or two. It would have been too easy to quit. But I could commit to and handle thirty days and work out every single day no matter what. After thirty days, I had more energy, felt better, and felt stronger. Deciding I wanted to feel that way more, I recommitted. My birthday is April 1st, so I decided if I could make it for one month, I could do two more months and commit to working out every day until my birthday. That's three months of working out every day. The last month was a lot easier than the first because I had started to create a new habit. And at that point, it was harder to miss a day than to make it. It felt great.

The following four steps are how you create change in your life:

1. Believe that changing your lifestyle will improve the quality of your health and life
2. Find out what motivates you and decide to change
3. Make a goal
4. Commit and take action!

Don't bite off more than you can chew but don't sell yourself short either. It's easier than you think. Go for it! Dream big! Imagine the life and future you want for yourself and then make it happen!

CHAPTER 6

Setting Clearly
Defined Goals

*"If you want to be happy, set a goal
that commands your thoughts, liberates
your energy, and inspires your hopes."*
—Andrew Carnegie

Health is not a goal; it is a value. Health is not a destination; it is a lifelong journey. *CORE Principle #4: Health and healing take time and are a continuous process.* Health cannot be your goal. Instead, it is a *CORE Value.* Health is not a specific goal because we cannot even clearly define it. Goals must be clearly defined. If you do not know what you want and do not have clearly defined goals, then you will never know when you get there. We can't achieve health; that isn't a clearly defined goal. We can optimize our health. We can maximize our health. We can work toward having our bodies work at their optimum potential. But we can't achieve health.

Since health can be defined as the body's ability to adapt to its internal and external environment (*CORE Principle #5: The human body is adaptable*), your health can get better or worse but is never something that you achieve or accomplish. We tend to think we are healthy when we feel good, but that is not a good barometer. People can have cancer or heart disease for years without knowing it.

MY DAD—FEELING GOOD DOES NOT MEAN YOU ARE HEALTHY

One Sunday, I had gone over to visit my eighty-four-year-old dad, and he was bragging about how healthy he was. On Friday, he had gone to his doctor and was given a clean bill of health. He said that his heart was perfect. His lungs were perfect. All his numbers were perfect! He was excited! I celebrated with him for a while; however, I noticed that he struggled to even get out of his recliner and was very slow moving. Over the years, his agility and ability to move and get around had everything to do with his daily activities. He would go through phases where he would walk every day. He would go down to Snap Fitness and exercise. He would be focused on improving his health with daily, consistent habits. It was amazing to see how quickly things would improve for him. On the other hand, at times, he would become very sedentary. He would just sit in his recliner all day, every day, and watch TV. During those times, his level of function would decline rapidly. It was obvious that on that Sunday he had not been exercising. When I asked, he confirmed that he hadn't done any exercise or even gone for a walk in months. I gave him the big pep talk about how you can't judge your health based on how you feel or your numbers at your doctor's office. You can only judge your health based on your lifestyle. I encouraged him to set clearly defined goals that would keep him active and improve his health and quality of life. I suggested that he set a goal to walk for a specific amount of time five days per week. He was motivated. He went down to Snap Fitness the next morning and walked for forty minutes on the treadmill after having not done any walking for months. After his workout, while walking to his car, he had a heart attack. I felt horrible. However, at the emergency room, they found that two of his coronary arteries were 90 percent occluded. They even told him that it was probably good that he had this heart attack when he did because if his arteries had worsened and then he had a heart attack, it would have been worse, and he might not have survived it.

Did the treadmill cause his heart attack? Was it my pep talk that caused his heart attack? Did his coronary arteries get occluded over that weekend? Or is it possible that it was due to his lifestyle over a lifetime? Some people may be more susceptible to some health conditions than others, but can we just agree that how you live your life will impact how and when those conditions affect you? Just because you feel good and your doctor says all your health markers look good, doesn't mean you are healthy. You can only base your health on the quality of your lifestyle. It is important to set clearly defined goals to create a lifestyle that improves your health and quality of life.

Health can be quantified by the ability of your body to adapt to its internal and external environment. Health equals adaptability. It's that simple! The only question now is how to get your body to adapt as close as possible to its genetic potential. The truth is that we can all do better.

GOALS FOR A HEALTHIER LIFESTYLE

This is where goals come in. Quality, specific, well-defined goals will lead to healthier habits, and healthier habits become a healthier lifestyle and a healthier, happier, and more vital you. But you can't just set any goal. Remember that your goals need to be consistent with the work you're willing to do. Once you know what you are willing to do, you are ready to set your goals. Goals need to be specific. Saying you want to eat more salad is not a goal. Setting a goal to have a salad for lunch five days per week is a goal because it is specific. Setting a goal to drink more water is not a goal. Setting a goal to drink 120 oz. per day is a goal. You could very easily make a goal to go to bed at the same time and get up at the same time. That is specific.

Your goals also need to be attainable. To be attainable, give yourself a little break. Set the goal to go to bed at the same time and get up at the same time five days a week instead of every day. Otherwise, you set yourself up for failure. Remember, we are striving for improvement, not perfection. Decide what your body needs, and then make your goals specific, meaningful, and attainable for you.

Be specific about what you are going to do for exercise and make it something that is attainable for you. If your goal is not something you can do or are willing to do, you have just set yourself up for failure. As soon as people begin to fail at their goals, their human nature is to abandon their goals. So, as you set goals to begin your new healthier lifestyle, don't bite off more than you can chew. People fill the gyms in January with their New Year's resolutions, but by March, they are already empty. Don't be one of those people.

SECTION 3

Lifestyle Changes for Living the CORE Life

"An empty lantern provides no light. Self-care is the fuel that allows your light to shine brightly."
—Unknown

In order to improve your health, you need to address all areas of health with the same *CORE Principles*:

- Diet
- Exercise
- Sleep
- Stress
- Emotional/mental health
- Relationships
- Body composition
- Healthy spine and nervous system

In each category of health, think of goals that will help you increase nutrients and decrease toxins. It's that simple! You need to reflect on every category if you genuinely want to improve your health and avoid chronic disease.

CHAPTER 7

Diet

*"Our food should be our medicine, and
our medicine should be our food."*
—Hippocrates

An old adage says, "You are what you eat." There is some truth to that. What you eat and drink make the building blocks of your body. But that's just the tip of the iceberg. Everything we ingest impacts the production of hormones, proteins, and enzymes, which in turn impacts your body's ability to function. Thus, how we eat, what we eat, and when we eat all affect our health and not just whether we are fat or skinny. Our diet affects our energy, our mental clarity, how we sleep, and even our immune function.

Many leading experts will tell you that our bodily functions are controlled and regulated by our hormones and that the organ responsible for producing a certain hormone regulates the production of that hormone. Growth and height are regulated by the growth hormone, which is produced by the pituitary gland. Blood sugars are regulated by insulin and glucagon, which are produced by the pancreas. Sexual maturation is regulated by testosterone and estrogen, which are produced by the ovaries and testes. Body temperature is regulated by the thyroid-stimulating hormone and free thyroxin. The list goes on and on. Because of this, if someone has too much or too little of a given hormone, experts give the body something from the outside (a drug) to alter the function of the gland responsible for that hormone's production.

However, there is a problem with this thinking. This is the outside-in, mechanistic, allopathic medical model that we have all been accustomed to. If this is what we believe, it affects everything we do to influence our health. Remember, *the CORE Life* is based on universal principles. *CORE Principle #1:* **The human body is self-healing, self-regulating, and self-maintaining, and there is an inborn, innate intelligence that runs, regulates, coordinates, and regenerates every organ and system of the body.**

Yes, hormones do affect function, but there is a question that isn't being asked: "What controls which hormones get produced, how much of each hormone should be produced, how fast, and where do they get sent?" We know this is our innate intelligence. For example, the nervous system sends signals to the brain through afferent nerves to communicate how much sugar is in the bloodstream. The brain integrates that information, then sends a signal back through efferent nerves to tell the pancreas how much insulin to produce. If someone dies, they still have a brain and they still have a pancreas, but there is no intelligence to tell the pancreas what to do. So, they can't give all the blame to the pancreas for producing too much or too little. When they do, the only option is to give the body a drug to alter the function of that gland. This is a big mistake, and one of the biggest reasons for our continued declining health.

Instead, we need to combat the issues from the inside out, giving our body more of what it needs and avoiding the things that are toxic to it so Innate can do its job to keep your body functioning at its best. Since this is a guide to simplify healthy living, I am not going to give you a specific diet plan or recipe book. Instead, I will address a few principles. Nature got it right, and the more educated a species is, the further they get from living an innate life. Most species have no other choice but to live innately. Birds fly south in the winter. Salmon swim upstream to spawn. They don't wake up in the morning and check the weather app and decide which day would be ideal or when they think it would be the most convenient. They just go because they are driven by their innate intelligence. They listen to their instincts. Because humans use more of their educated brains, we have moved further from using our innate brains for thinking and problem solving. If nature did get it right, then we should look at what the human species is really designed to eat and live by those principles.

DIET PRINCIPLES TO LIVE BY

Instead of outlining a diet you should follow, I want you to develop principles to live your life by. That is what *the CORE Life* is all about: healthy, simple, core principles.

Drink more water. I am talking about the clear, pure stuff. Don't try to convince yourself that since juice, soda, coffee, alcohol, or anything else you drink has water in it, you are drinking water. Even though it is true, your body needs the pure stuff. Don't put anything in your water to flavor it or carbonate it either. Just drink the pure stuff, and drink lots of it. It is one of our body's most important nutrients, and we need a lot of it.

Stop eating sugar. Sugar is a poison to our bodies, and we eat way too much of it, as it is in almost everything that is processed. That's how they keep us buying and eating it. Sugar comes in many forms, so don't be fooled, as starches are basically sugar too. Remember, sugar is basically glucose, and starches are just long chains of glucose. So, most breads and pastas do the same thing as eating a lot of sugar. Stop eating sugar.

During college, I drank a lot of Dr Pepper. Then, during midterms and finals, I would ramp it up to Jolt Cola. I can still remember their jingle: "All the sugar and twice the caffeine for those who dare to want it all." As a college student, I definitely wanted it all! It was like they were challenging me to drink the worst product that they could possibly get away with making and selling, and I was all in. At some point after I graduated college, I stopped drinking soda altogether. I replaced it with just drinking water, and it was crazy watching the belly fat just melt off me. Most people don't realize how much their food and drink choices impact their life and health.

In working with thousands of people over the last several decades and investigating their lifestyles, I am continually shocked at how much people justify their choices. They will justify drinking tons of zero-calorie or diet sodas because they say that they don't have sugar in them. It isn't just that sugar is bad for us but the massive quantities that we consume create insulin resistance. These diet drinks have a similar effect on blood sugar levels and insulin resistance as well as being toxic to the nervous system. These drinks are just as chemically toxic to the human body, if not more toxic, and making any attempt to justify these drinks as a healthy choice will still leave you responsible for the consequences. If you choose to drink that junk, just do it knowing that it is a horrible choice, and you have to accept the consequences of it. No excuses!

Avoid processed foods. There it is! It's that simple! I have never seen a healthy diet plan teach people to drink less water, eat more sugar, or eat more processed foods. A few diet plans do teach people to eat their premade processed products to lose weight, but they aren't healthy diet plans. There is nothing healthy about a diet consisting of processed food like lemon bars and chocolate smoothies. You may lose weight consuming those, but don't try to convince yourself you're making a healthy choice.

A healthy diet should consist of mostly meat, eggs, vegetables, fruit, berries, nuts, seeds, and healthy fats. Beyond that, it comes down to the quality of the food, how much of it you eat, and when you eat it.

I honestly don't eat that disciplined, but I live with principles and don't make excuses. If I eat fast food one day or a candy bar or bowl of ice cream, I own it. It's not the end of the world. I don't beat myself up over it, and I don't make excuses for it. I just decided that I was going to focus on healthy eating, and as I did so and continue to do so, I allow a little indulgence here or there. But if I start to feel like my body isn't healthy. I don't make excuses. I created the body I have, so I can change it if I want to.

Since I believe that nature got it right, it makes the most sense to me to look at how our ancestors ate before the agriculture and dairy industry got involved. There is a reason we have so much gluten intolerance and lactose intolerance today, and it is man-made. If you add the FDA and the massive marketing campaigns that the food industry pushes on the public, it is clear why we have so much chronic illnesses and diseases. It is not only understandable but also predictable. If you can just sit back and look at the big picture, it really makes sense why we are so unhealthy and getting worse. When you combine the food industry with the pharmaceutical industry, we don't have a fighting chance—unless we take back our power. ***CORE Principle #2: You are responsible for your life and health!***

CHAPTER 8

Exercise

"Get a daily workout, and you will naturally eat and sleep better. You will be a different person. Exercise will enhance your performance in your daily hours."
—John Soforic

Just like you will find many different theories on what to eat and how often to eat, experts have mixed opinions on exercise. Many of the leading experts disagree and each supports their theories with research, making it hard to know what is true.

The only thing not up for debate is that the human body needs regular, consistent exercise to be as healthy as possible.

Since we don't know the exact formula for exercise and since it is likely that each person would have different needs, *the CORE Life* recognizes certain fundamental principles to live by instead of an exact list of do this, not that. You are responsible, so don't make excuses.

THREE TYPES OF EXERCISE

Exercise can be broken down into three basic types: stretching, strengthening, and cardiovascular. All three are important.

Younger people tend to get more exercise than older people. Whether through sports or other forms of playing, kids generally get more exercise—although, over the past few decades, kids are now becoming more and more sedentary. As adults, exercise either happens with a physical job, being involved in hobbies or sports that provide exercise, or consciously choosing to exercise. However, sadly, most don't exercise regularly, and those that do, don't exercise enough or they don't engage in all three types. Instead, they walk or run three times per week, or go to a yoga or Pilates class, or a boot camp, or walk on a treadmill. This isn't the best choice for optimizing your health potential. I don't want to minimize the benefits of these types of exercise because they have awesome benefits. However, strengthening and cardiovascular exercise are also important.

At the gym, younger people engage more in strength training, while older people tend to do more cardiovascular exercise. Yet, as people age, it is even more important for them to do strength training for optimal health.

It is also important to stretch, which most people don't do enough.

My wife Zan is a constant inspiration for me, especially when it comes to exercise. She exercises to stay healthy, to look good, to feel good, to decrease stress, and I believe as a form of meditation for her. She will go to the gym to ride a bike or use an elliptical machine or arc trainer while she reads. She exercises as a way of life. She gets up early in the morning to exercise for an hour, even if she has a poor night's sleep. If she has time later, she will go for a bike ride or go to the gym to work out again and read. It is harder for her to miss a day than to make it every day. Even when she is sick, she will try to work out most of the time with the belief that it might help her feel better or burn out the virus. She is so humble about it too. It is no different for her than sleeping. She sleeps every day, and she exercises every day. If I set a goal to exercise every day for thirty days or ninety days, I make a big deal about it when I do it. I act like I just ran a marathon or hit some major milestone in my life and want to shout it from a mountaintop. Zan, on the other hand, could work out every day for a year or two, and you would never even hear about it. It is just who she is, not what she does. This is the way it should be for all of us. Exercise should be no different from getting sleep or drinking water. It is one of our basic needs.

EXERCISE PRINCIPLES TO LIVE BY

Break a sweat every day. Our bodies are designed to move. Cardiovascular exercise is important, as it keeps our heart and lungs working at their best, which is necessary to keep everything else working at its best. Some people say they need one day of rest per week, so they don't exercise on that day. But it is OK to exercise every day. If you choose to take a break from exercising one day, that is fine. But understand this doesn't mean you lie around on the couch and watch TV all day, even if it is only one day per week. If you choose to do that, fine. It is your choice! Just don't make the excuse that it is the healthiest choice. Rest is important for health and for our muscles to recover; however, no one needs to spend twenty-four consecutive hours lounging in bed or on a couch for great health. It's OK to exercise every day. In fact, it's a **CORE Principle**.

Stretch. Stretching exercises should be included with every workout. Yoga practice is great on many levels beyond just the flexibility it creates. Whether you include yoga as part of your exercise routine or not, you need to stretch in some way every day. As we age, we tend to lose flexibility, decreasing our ability to function at our best, making us more susceptible to injuries, and decreasing our quality of life. Stretching will help prevent that.

Lift weights. If you don't use it, you lose it! Too many older people are unable to care for themselves or get off the floor if they fall due to their weight and/or muscle weakness. Strength training will allow you to be more active and independent as you age. Another benefit of strength training is that your metabolism will continue to run higher for the days following your workout, burning more fat as your muscles recover. Strength training is important for everyone but becomes even more important as we age.

CHAPTER 9

Sleep

"Sleep is like the golden chain that binds
our health and body together."
—*Thomas Dekker*

The quality of your sleep has a significant impact on the quality of your health. Even if you only sleep for six hours per night, that is 25 percent of your life that you spend sleeping. If you sleep eight hours per night, that is a third of your life. With it taking up so much of your life, it is clearly important!

THREE FACTORS OF SLEEP

When it comes to sleep, three factors are important:

- Quality
- Quantity
- Consistency

(By the way, these factors are important for the other categories as well.)

Quality. Yes, you have more direct control over quantity and consistency, while quality is harder to control. If you decide to go to bed at the same time and get up at the same time, assuming you don't have a sleep disorder, this takes care of the quantity and consistency parts. But just because quality is harder to control doesn't mean you can't improve the quality of your sleep. You can impact the quality of your sleep based on your lifestyle. You can't compare yourself to anyone else; however, you can improve yourself by doing more good and less bad. Refer to **CORE Principle #3:** *If you give your body more of what it needs and avoid more of the things that are toxic to it, you will become healthier.*

Following these principles improve the quality of your sleep:

- A good bed is important. A great bed can be expensive, and, like most things, you get what you pay for. If you buy a cheap bed, you get a cheap bed. Invest in a quality bed. You spend a lot of time there, and it is important.
- Invest in a quality pillow.
- Sleep on your back or your side. Stomach sleeping is bad for your health.
- Live a healthy lifestyle (which is explained in the previous categories and the categories coming up).

Quantity. Too much or too little sleep can create stress on the body, which reduces our overall health potential. However, even the experts debate how much we need. A general guideline is that seven–eight hours per night is ideal for most people. We have all heard of people that get by on four–five hours per night, but even if they are "getting by," they aren't making a healthy choice. Without getting enough sleep, the human body doesn't have enough time for rest, recovery, regeneration, and repair.

The reason we can't really say exactly how many hours you need is partly that we all have different needs due to our genetics, our environment, our lifestyle, and our stressors, etc., and partly because your quality of sleep impacts how much you need. If someone gets great quality sleep, they will need less quantity. Someone that gets poor-quality sleep will need more quantity. And even then, individual needs may change depending on what is going on in their life at that time. When someone is fighting an illness or recovering from an injury, they may need more sleep. If they are going through a lot of stress, either physically or emotionally, they may need more sleep.

Consistency. The body works in circadian rhythms. This is a natural internal process regulating the sleep-wake cycle that repeats every twenty-four hours. So, it helps your body to continue to regulate this if you always go to bed at the same time and wake up at the same time. If you don't, you risk throwing off your circadian rhythms and putting your body in a stressful state. The closer we can live to embracing the natural, innate processes of the body, the healthier we will be. Working a night shift has been shown to have many negative health effects due to disrupting the body's natural circadian rhythms, including, diabetes, heart disease, obesity, and many more.

THE NEED FOR BETTER SLEEP

Sleep centers, over the past several decades, have popped up all over the world. Due to massive amounts of sleep studies now being performed every day, we have a much better idea of how serious and prevalent sleep problems are. According to *The Lancet Respiratory Medicine*, an estimated 936 million adults aged 30–69 years of age have moderate to severe obstructive sleep apnea globally.[4] Sleep problems are very common and have a detrimental effect on our health. Here is the good news: eat better, exercise better, give yourself the proper quantity and consistency of sleep, and do better in all the categories coming up, and you will have better quality sleep. The other option is to feel like a victim and tell yourself, "This is my lot in life, and it's totally out of my control." *CORE Principle #2: You are responsible for your life and health.* The choice is yours!

[4] Adam V Benjafield, PhD, et.al, "Estimation of the Global Prevalence and Burden of Obstructive Sleep Apnoea: A Literature-Based Analaysis," *The Lancet Respiratory Medicine* 7, no.8 (July 2019): 687–98, https://doi.org/10.1016/S2213-2600(19)30198-5.

CHAPTER 10

Stress

"Stress is not what happens to us. It is our response to what happens. And response is something we can choose."
—*Maureen Killoran*

Stress has been linked to almost every health condition we know of. Most people know this, but because they don't fully understand stress, they let it get the best of them and feel like a victim of it. You have more control over your stress levels than you think. It starts with understanding it.

UNDERSTANDING STRESS

Stress has many positive effects and is important for a healthy life: it is necessary to increase muscle growth and can cause you to move or work harder or faster. A lot of records broken in the biggest events, like the Olympics, Superbowl, or other championships, are partly because of stress. Have you ever had a lot to do before you could leave on vacation and somehow managed to get two weeks' worth of work done in just two days? You had no choice but to move faster, work harder, and be more efficient. Having deadlines does this to us. As a procrastinator in school, I am well aware of this principle. I would too often wait until right before the test to cram, putting myself under intense stress. I did well, but it didn't need to be so stressful. It was self-induced.

Yes, stress in the short term helps us perform better, but in the long term, it is deadly! Being able to get two weeks' worth of work done in two days is great if you then have a chance to let go, rest, recharge, and recuperate. However, if someone goes from one deadline to the next, it takes a toll on their health. That sustained, prolonged stress is extremely hard on the body. It leads to a lot of chronic health conditions and poor body function. Thus, it is important to understand how the body **adapts** to stress and use this to our benefit, in order to maximize our health potential. When we are under stress, it physiologically affects all of us in the same way. It shifts our body from parasympathetic dominant to sympathetic dominant, causing us to go into fight or flight mode. When that happens, there is an increase in stress hormones. A lot of our vital systems shut down partially to force energy and blood supply to our muscles. This is why people under stress have higher blood pressure, increased heart rate, and increased muscle tension. In a parasympathetic state, our bodies function better. This is when our bodies can heal and regenerate the best and fastest. This is also why rest and sleep are so important. By understanding this principle, you can make changes in your lifestyle to improve the negative effects of stress. The other option is to remain feeling like a victim of your stress and let it destroy your health.

HOW TO REDUCE STRESS

Rest. Make sure you take time to power down every day. Some people are busy all day at work just to race home and busy themselves with home stuff, and then crash just to start over the next day. It is important to find some time during the day to *power down*. Whether that means taking a power nap at lunch or even engaging in a short meditation, you just need to find a quiet place to *power down*. If you need to, go to your car, put the seat down, close your eyes, and breathe. If you don't get the time during the day, then do it on your way home. Stop in a parking lot, close your eyes, relax, and breathe. This shifts your body from the hindbrain, primitive, reactive, sympathetic dominant, fight or flight state to a forebrain, relaxed, proactive, parasympathetic dominant, high-functioning state. By choosing to take specific actions, you can change the hormones being produced in your body and, in turn, shift the negative effects to positive ones. It's important. Power down!

Start your day right. How you start your day affects the rest of your day. Some people wake in the morning and immediately start their stressful day—either checking emails, racing to get ready for work, or getting kids ready for school. If you start your day in a stressful state, you immediately go into that sympathetic dominant, reactive state we just talked about. In other words, if you wake up in the morning and immediately start getting ready for work or doing housework, or making breakfast, etc., you get an increase in stress hormones and that pattern stays throughout your day—unless you take time to power down. You should give yourself extra time in the morning to do relaxing things, so you don't start your day in a state of stress. You could start with meditation, exercise, visualization, affirmations, etc., which will produce an entirely different set of hormones in your body, allowing you to function in a much more creative, proactive, high-functioning, and productive way. Remember, you can feel like a victim or make better choices. The choice is yours!

Meditate. Whether you do this first thing in the morning or while powering down at lunch or in the evening, meditation will help decrease stress hormones and improve your health. You can find many forms of meditation, but most of them include clearing your mind and focusing on breathing. Both are valuable tools to reduce stress, or at least the negative effects of stress.

Diet, exercise, and sleep. We already talked about these, but it is important to understand that a healthy diet, regular exercise, and quality sleep decrease the allostatic load of stress and improve your health and quality of life. When your body has a decrease in stress, it can adapt better and faster. This is the definition of health.

Stop procrastinating. Procrastination is a part of human nature, or maybe I'm just saying that to make myself feel better. We procrastinate all kinds of things: completing a task we need to do, handling an issue in a relationship, and sending an email or text message that we need to send. Maybe you are upset with a friend or coworker, but instead of having the conversation that you need to have or make the apology that you need to make, you spend days or weeks carrying around the stress and negativity with you, replaying the tapes of what happened and making up your own stories of what the other person is thinking or saying. This is why it has been said that "procrastination is the thief of health." This is true for many reasons. Some people wait until they are sick and unhealthy to start focusing on their health, which can be too late. The truth is, no matter where you are in your life, it's important to start focusing on your health *now*. The best way to avoid sickness and disease is to create a healthy body. Another reason is that when you procrastinate anything, you create more stress, leading to higher levels of stress hormones. Increasing this allostatic load causes chronic long-term stress, which leads to chronic long-term health problems.

LIVING ON THE TOP HALF OF YOUR TANK

When my oldest daughter Bri got her driver's license and had been driving for about a year, I noticed that she always had under a quarter tank of gas. That seemed stressful, so I asked her one day if she ever filled her tank all the way up. She laughed and said, "No! It's expensive." When I asked her how much gas she would put in when she went to the gas station, she said, "About five or ten dollars." I wondered how often she was running late for school and was worried about running out of gas. I could picture her having to decide if she should get gas and just be late for school or hurry to school and risk running out of gas. That's a stressful way to live. Her tank was never above a half tank. Essentially, she was living on the bottom of her tank. One Christmas, I gave her a gas card to fill up her tank. I sent her a video telling her to fill up her gas tank all the way, but I was only gifting her the top half. The bottom half belonged to me. She could only use the gas on the top half, meaning a half tank was now her new empty. I challenged her to go get gas sometimes when it was above three-fourths of a tank. I explained this principle to her: When you aren't pressed for time, keep it full. If your tank is always full, you just reduced stress in one area of your life. She used the excuse that gas is expensive, but she was spending the same amount of money on gas. She was just replacing the bottom five dollars instead of the top five dollars.

Have you ever needed to print something, but you were out of ink and didn't have time to get more—you needed it now? That's stressful! Living your life on the top half of your tank means always keeping an extra ink cartridge on hand and getting new ink when you still have some left. What if you went through your entire life and looked at where you could live on the top half of your tank? This is a principle to live by. I challenge all of you to find all the places where you are living on the bottom half of the tank and change to living on the top half. Living this way is a belief system. Embracing this **CORE Principle** and making it a part of how you think and who you are will decrease stress in your life and is a major step in creating a healthy life for yourself with ease.

CHAPTER 11

Emotional and Mental Health

"Mental Health . . . is not a destination, but a process.
It's about how you drive, not where you are going."
—Noam Shpancer, PhD

Since our emotional and mental health play an important role in our overall health, I address how we can improve this area of our lives. When it comes to diet and exercise, most people know it is their choice in how well they do. They make excuses that they don't have time to exercise or that eating well is expensive, but they really do know that they are responsible for their actions. People just don't know, acknowledge, or respect the consequences of poor choices in those categories, but they do know it is a choice. When it comes to emotional/ mental health, many believe it is out of our control. Nope! We have more control than we know. If you eat better, exercise better, sleep better, and stress less (things most believe they can control), you will enjoy a better mental and emotional state. Can you see how they all build on each other? Besides the choice to improve in the other categories, you also can make other choices to improve your mental and emotional health.

Choices to Improve Your Mental Health

Make the choice to

- limit your time with negative people
- stop participating in negative gossip
- be more attracted to things and people that align with your new views
- read things and do things that inspire you and improve your quality of life
- find more purpose in your life
- have an attitude of gratitude

If you don't feel your life has meaning and purpose, you will find that focusing on your health and finding a passion for it is an inspiration for others and is meaningful.

One of our basic human needs is to live a life of purpose. It is a nutrient. Find a local cause to donate your time. Do something that serves a purpose greater than yourself. When you choose an empowering belief system and live your life by it, when you focus on taking the best care of yourself, and when you find a purpose greater than yourself, your emotional/mental state will improve, along with your overall health and quality of life.

It is important to realize that focusing time and money on your own emotional health is not selfish. It is actually the opposite. When you are healthier, you will have much more to give to your family, friends, and whatever you find purpose in. When you lose your health, your entire life will become consumed by it. This does not have a positive effect on your family and friends. Spending your time, energy, and money focusing on all aspects of your health will also have a positive effect on all those people you know and love.

GRATITUDE

Since gratitude is probably the most important thing you can do to improve your emotional/mental state, I want to expound on it. Some people are naturally grateful. They feel gratitude every day for everything. But for some reason, it seems to be human nature for people to take things for granted. Yet we have so much to be grateful for. When you are truly in a state of gratitude, it is impossible to also be in a state of fear, anger, negativity, or hate, and you can't feel like a victim.

So take time to engage daily in activities that increase your gratitude:

- Plan time to journal what you are grateful for
- Do gratefulness meditations. If you can't think of things that you are grateful for, find guided gratitude meditations on YouTube. There are lots of them to choose from

Gratitude will take you out of sympathetic (fight or flight) dominance and put you into parasympathetic dominance. Start and end each day with gratitude. It is good for your soul. It is good for your health.

CHAPTER 12

Relationships and Social Life

"Treasure your relationships, not your possessions."
—Anthony J. D'Angelo

Just like purpose is a nutrient, so is love. It is important to have meaningful relationships. This can be with a spouse/significant other, family, and/or friends. It also means you need to have a healthy relationship with yourself. You should have all of them. If you don't, you should be actively pursuing them all. **CORE *Principle #2: You are responsible for your life and health.*** You are no longer the victim. If you are telling yourself "I'm not worthy of a loving relationship," "people don't like me," "I don't like people," "my kids don't want to spend time with me," or any other negative victim self-talk, stop it. Fix it! It's important for your health and quality of life. I know I sound like it is easy to just change the way you think or feel, but I do know that it isn't that easy. I just want you to know you don't have to accept it. You don't have to let it own you. You are in charge of yourself.

It all starts with having an awareness that it is a problem and is affecting your health, then deciding that you want it to be better. Just like everything else, visualize the outcome you want, figure out what you need to make that happen, set clear, achievable goals, and then go after it. Make it happen. Remember, you aren't striving for perfection, but improvement. I think everyone can do a little better.

RELATIONSHIPS TO FOCUS ON

Yourself. Many people have a hard time being alone. Because many people have negative self-talk, they busy themselves with their home life, their work life, or with friends to avoid spending time alone with themselves in their own thoughts. Making time for personal time is important for your health.

You can do a few activities to improve your relationship with yourself:

- Meditation
- Gratitude journaling
- Positive affirmations
- Exercise—hiking, biking, swimming, weight training, etc.

Your spouse/significant other. Once the honeymoon phase is over in a relationship, it is important to make a conscious effort to maintain connection. My wife Zan and I have four kids. Between work and taking care of the kids, it is easy for time to slip by without spending enough quality time together to maintain a great connection. We have found that dedicating one night a week to date night has made a big difference. It allows us time with just the two of us to catch up without any other distractions. We get to know how the other person is feeling, what they've been learning about themselves and life itself, and so much more. It is a highlight of my week. I always look forward to it, and together we always make sure it happens. If something is more urgent on that night, we do it on a different night because it's a commitment. It's a commitment to ourselves and our relationship. At least once every two months, we make time to get away for a night or a weekend romantic getaway. We don't have to go far, and oftentimes we just get a hotel in town. Once people lose connection, it is sometimes hard to get it back. The joy of a healthy relationship strengthens your health, and the stress of an unhealthy relationship causes you to become sick.

Friends. Having friends and a healthy social life is important for your health. It is a basic human need, a nutrient, to have community and human connection. If you don't have friends that you spend time with, find hobbies or things that you're interested in and develop friendships with people that have similar interests. When you're having fun with friends or doing things that you love doing, it decreases the stress levels in your body and improves your overall health.

If you have great relationships, don't take them for granted. Strive to strengthen them, as they are one of the most important things we have in this world and one of the most important reasons to make our health a priority. The healthier we are, the more we have to give to our relationships. The unhealthier we are, the more of a drain it can be on our relationships. Once again, it's our choice how much we prioritize it.

CHAPTER 13

Body Composition

"Take care of your body. It's the only
place you have to live."
—Jim Rohn

Body composition is just a look at what makes up your body. Most body composition analyzers test how much of your body is made up of fat, how much water, and how much muscle. Recently, the media has talked a lot about body image. Oprah has been an influencer since the eighties. When she was on a weight loss kick, she inspired millions to live a healthier lifestyle. In fact, when she did Weight Watchers, the stock shot up. When she gained all the weight back and more, the storyline changed to body image, loving yourself, and accepting your body. While she probably had great intentions, I don't think everyone got the right message. What I saw was a lot of overweight people jumping on the bandwagon to feel validated for their unhealthy lifestyle. You should love yourself, no matter where you are in your life, but please take an honest look at how you are living your life and take responsibility for the outcome. Whether you take responsibility or you don't, you are still responsible.

I'm not going to pull any punches here. When a high percentage of a person's body is made up of fat, their body cannot work at its best. We could just stop there. What more is there to say? We need fat, but too much is unhealthy. I love the message that we should all love ourselves, but supporting the lifestyle that has led to people being so overweight is just wrong. Obesity is now considered a diagnosed disease, leading people to feel like a victim. This takes away all their power. It may seem easier to believe that it's your lot in life and you are a victim of it, saying "I just have a disease." I don't mean to make light of this, but couldn't everyone do a little better? Couldn't we all try a little harder? Couldn't we all find some places in our lives to make better choices? Isn't this a better way to live your life? ***CORE Principle #3: If you give your body more of what it needs and avoid more of the things that are toxic to it, you will become healthier.***

Let me put our society's mentality into perspective. During COVID-19, people raided the grocery stores. Some people's entire cart was loaded with pastries, ice cream, soda, and Fruit Loops, yet they were terrified of COVID-19. They should be terrified of their lifestyle. Can you see the absurdity? They masked up, scared of getting a disease, yet they were living on fourteen lifestyle drugs (drugs people take for conditions created by their lifestyle) and continuing to live the lifestyle that created it. If we had more healthy people, we wouldn't have to be so terrified of sickness.

If you live a healthy lifestyle by doing more good and less bad, your body will find a healthy weight for you. Whatever that is, love yourself! Always be honest with yourself about the lifestyle you are living and if you could do a little better. If you want better, do better. Your body composition matters! Don't make excuses.

▌INBODY CHALLENGE

I purchased the InBody 570 earlier this year for testing body composition in my office. I intend to use it for testing in a new business I am opening this next year, called **CORE Life Transformation**. When I first got it, I weighed 208 lbs. and was 22 percent body fat. I decided to set up a twelve-week challenge for myself, focusing on losing weight and fat. I wanted to retain muscle, but I was willing to sacrifice some to lose the weight and fat. I set a goal to get down to 185 lbs. and under 15 percent body fat. When I hit those goals with time to spare, I reset my goals. Since I had graduated high school at 178 lbs., I decided that would be a good goal. I went for it, with a goal of 178 lbs. and 12 percent body fat. I ended the twelve weeks down 30 lbs. and at 13 percent body fat. I lost 22 lbs. of fat. I had sacrificed 7 lbs. of muscle in the process, but it was just a challenge. After the challenge, I worked on gaining muscle back and was less concerned with gaining weight and body fat, as long as I had a healthy body composition.

Can you see that I didn't feel like a victim? I knew I could decide what I wanted and then make it happen if I chose to. We can all do that. Just decide what you want and make sure it is attainable based on the work you are willing to put into it. Set goals. And then, take action and make it happen! It's an empowering way to live.

It is not just having a healthy body composition that makes you healthy. It is the lifestyle that is creating a healthy body composition. Everything in your life gets better when you create a healthier body. You need to make health your hobby. It should be something you are passionate about. Remember, you get to choose your attitude. Take your power back! Choose to love getting healthy.

If you hate to exercise or eat well, then change your perception of it. Don't feel like a victim of it. Transform your mind first, then you can transform your body, and this will, in turn, transform your life.

CHAPTER 14

Your Spine, Posture, and Nervous System

"Look well to the spine for the cause of disease."
—*Hippocrates*

Your spine houses and protects your nervous system. The alignment and function of your spine have a direct impact on your nervous system and the ability of your nervous system to properly regulate your body. This is almost completely ignored by our medical system. If someone has enough damage to their nervous system that it completely shuts down function, only then is it addressed. The human body is not that black and white, though. It is not all or nothing. Just like an electrical current, it is variable based on the source of the power, what the current is being transmitted over, and what is receiving the current. The source of the power provides the maximum potential that could be received by the receiver. It is then only limited by what the current is being transmitted over and the quality of the receiver. For simplicity purposes, let's look at an audio system. Let's just say that you have the best source known to man sending the signal to the best speakers that money can buy. But if you have a cheap speaker wire, the sound quality will be poor, as you are now limited to the maximum potential of the speaker wire. Now, let's say you have the best possible source sending the signal through the best speaker wire that money can buy, but you have a cheap speaker. The maximum potential is now limited to the quality of the speaker.

Let's look at the same scenario related to the human body.

The source of the power is your brain. Innate intelligence travels through the nervous system from your brain (the source) to your body. The current, or mental impulse, is being transmitted over the nervous system (the wire) to the organs and systems (the speaker). The quality of your health (the sound) would depend on the quality of all three parts. We know the source is the best it can be, always performing at 100 percent. Nature got it right. We can't make it any better. If the quality of the source is 100 percent, then we must then look at how the mental impulse (wire) is transmitted and the health of your body (the speaker). If you have an unhealthy body that you created through poor choices (lifestyle), you are then limited to the maximum health potential of that unhealthy body (the speaker).

We know our source (innate intelligence) is performing at 100 percent, so let's now assume you are doing everything you can, through living a healthy lifestyle, and taking good care of your physical body, so your systems and organs are working at their best. The only variable now is your nervous system (wire) and your spine is what houses and protects it. Your nervous system is the connection between your brain and your body. Since your spinal cord and spinal nerves travel through the spine, it is important for your spine to be healthy to prevent interference with the nervous system. If the spine is misaligned or not functioning properly, it creates interference with the mental impulse or signals being sent from the brain to the body. Even minor, undetectable disturbances with the nervous system can have a significant effect on the ability of the body to adapt properly. A person may or may not have back or neck pain associated with this interference, but it reduces the ability of the body to function properly.

Most people only address spinal health when they hurt and then the only objective is to get rid of the pain. Because it is so misunderstood and minimized, one of the most important things I would like for everyone to take away from this book is the importance of a healthy spine for a healthy body and healthy life. So you need to actively pursue keeping your spine in the best possible shape to prevent any unnecessary interference to the nerve signal/mental impulse from the brain to the body.

POSTURE

Many of us were told from the time we were young to sit up or stand up straight. I had always thought they said this just because it didn't look good to slouch. I didn't know the negative health implications of poor posture until I became a chiropractor. It is unfortunate that more people don't know the impact poor posture is having on their health. It is not easy to maintain good posture in our current lifestyles. It is hard enough to maintain good posture, but when you add cell phones, computers, etc., it is extremely challenging. It's also challenging to eat well, exercise regularly, drink enough water, and sleep well. Most people don't even consider posture, spinal function, or the nervous system when talking about important things to do to improve your health. Let me set the record straight. It is one of the most important things!

Let's just look for a moment at the negative effects of poor posture on your health.

Lungs: Would you agree that breathing is important for your health? One of the negative effects of poor posture is decreased lung capacity. What happens if you have decreased lung capacity? Do you think this has a negative effect on your health? Decreased lung capacity puts you at risk for heart disease, stroke, cancer, and most other chronic health conditions. You need oxygen in all the cells of the body for proper function and regeneration. It is an important nutrient.

Try falling into a slouch for a minute. Then try to take a deep breath. You can't! It is impossible to take a full breath without good posture because it restricts your ribcage from expanding and compresses your lungs and forces you to become a shallow breather. Oxygenation is an important nutrient to all your cells, organs, and tissues. It is necessary not only for function but for regeneration. Decreased lung capacity leads to weak and degenerating organs. If you lose your posture, it speeds up the aging process. If you improve your posture, it slows down the aging process.

Nervous system: Another major and even more important impact that poor posture has is the effect it has on the nervous system. When people have a forward-head posture, it causes tension in the spinal cord, which affects the information being transmitted over the nervous system, altering communication from the brain to the body. This is why it is so important to have proper spinal alignment. It is necessary for the optimal adaptation and function of all the organs and systems in the body. A forward-head posture can certainly come from a lifetime of sitting, standing, and lying poorly. However, in most cases, it comes from a lifetime of traumas and injuries. Whether they are minor or major, if these injuries are not corrected, they have a cumulative impact over time. Poor posture makes existing spinal problems worse. When you already have a problem in your spine and then put it under more stress, it gets worse.

Spine Damage

After taking thousands of X-rays over my three-plus decades of practice, I have seen many seemingly healthy people with seemingly good posture have uncorrected damage in their spine. Why? Because there has been little global education about the importance of healthy spine function to maintain healthy nerve function. If the spine issues do not require surgery, often the problems are considered to be just muscular in nature. This is just not true. People are being told that the muscles are what control the alignment and function of the spine, so they just need to strengthen the muscles around their spine. But the muscles just hold you upright and create movement; they don't control your alignment and function.

Imagine a door. Let's say that you attach a bungee cord to the doorknob to act like the muscle. It is the force that will cause the door to open or close. Would it change the alignment of the door or how the door moves if you attached the other end of the bungee cord to the floor or ceiling? Absolutely not. The bungee cord (muscle) determines when the door moves or how far, but it is the hinges on the door that determine the alignment and how the door moves. The hinges are like the ligaments, joint capsules, and disc tissue in the spine.

Let's say that the door is ajar. Moving the bungee cord to the ceiling or floor will never correct the alignment or function of the door. This is where you must do something to affect the hinges (ligaments, joint capsules, and disc tissue). We will talk later about what you can do, but it is important that you do the right thing for the right problem, or you are just wasting time, energy, and money without correcting the underlying problems.

The average thirteen-year-old child has had over a thousand significant traumas to their spine. It starts with the birth process. Just take both of your hands, interlace your fingers, and push down on your head. Now, do that for two hours. Or maybe five or six hours. Imagine the length of time some babies spend in labor with their mom pushing. Imagine this fragile little baby trying to be pushed through the birth canal. Would you ever take your newborn baby and push down on their head like that? Can you even imagine doing it with the same force as labor for as long as labor takes? Have you ever been sitting in a prolonged position for a long period of time, and when you stand up or straighten up, you feel stiff and maybe some pain? Imagine a tiny fetus in utero for months in a flexed position, and then during labor having their heads pulled into an extended position. Imagine having a doctor latch on with a vacuum extractor to pull the baby through the birth canal by its head into an extended position. Imagine the stress it must put that spine under.

I have checked and adjusted hundreds of newborn babies. I can't tell you how many times someone has asked, "Why would you adjust a tiny little newborn baby? They couldn't possibly need an adjustment yet." If people knew what I knew, it would be standard of care to have every baby checked for spinal alignment and function. The better question would be, "Why aren't they all being checked?" Remember, their health is dependent on it. Then, as the baby grows up, they experience numerous traumas that often get ignored:

- Falling off the couch or bed as a baby
- Tumbling down the stairs as a child
- Falling off the playground equipment
- Falling when they are learning to walk or ride a bike
- Getting injured while playing sports

When someone tells me they have never had a trauma, I know they have but just don't remember. Traumas happen to all of us, and we are an accumulation of the traumas we have had throughout our lives. Frequently these traumas cause people to have misalignments of their spine and often lose the normal curve in their neck, which can sometimes even cause a reversed curve. If this isn't corrected, it causes nerve interference and leads to spinal degeneration. Then add poor posture and life stresses, and these problems just get worse. In my experience, most of our spine problems started with uncorrected traumas when we are young. It is important that you seek out proper care when injuries occur, from childhood into your adulthood.

The CORE Life is all about living your life from the inside out. Life flows through the nervous system from the brain down and from the inside out. Since we live our lives through the nervous system, we must take care of our spines. Our health depends on it!

Innate Intelligence and the Nervous System

We know that an innate, inborn intelligence runs the body. *CORE Principle #1: The human body is self-healing, self-regulating, and self-maintaining, and there is an inborn, innate intelligence that runs, regulates, coordinates, and regenerates every organ and system of the body.* We believe that the center of control for this intelligence is the brain, which is in constant communication with every cell, organ, and tissue in the body. It is constantly receiving sensory input from the body, integrating that information, and creating the proper motor response to adapt to its environment. Remember, the ability of the body to properly adapt to its environment is how we defined health earlier. I know this is a simplified version of an extraordinarily complex system, but remember, the purpose of this book is to simplify health.

The center of control is the brain, but the brain is not the intelligence. This innate intelligence (life) is critical for our health. It is what causes the cells, organs, and tissues to adapt and regenerate. There is the information stored in the DNA of every cell to know exactly how we should adapt in every situation. It is that innate intelligence (life) that makes it happen. When someone dies, they still have the same number of brain cells, but they are no longer controlling and regulating the body. Their cells still have the DNA and information on how to adapt but no longer have life (innate intelligence) to take the information and make it happen. For the body to function at its best, it needs to be able to adapt to its internal and external environment.

This requires the nervous system to be healthy and functioning at its best. Even though the intelligence may be perfect, the quality of the information sent between the brain and the body depends on the quality of the signal being transmitted between the brain and the body through the nervous system. If anything interferes with the signal between your brain and body, you will experience suboptimal function and in many cases malfunction. When the organs and systems of the body can't adapt properly to internal and external stressors, then the body develops chronic health problems, sickness, and disease. When this happens, most people turn to their doctors for help. Those doctors look in their tool bag for a solution and write a prescription. The drugs we take have one purpose: to alter how our body is currently being regulated. When someone develops a health problem, it is almost always because the body is not adapting properly. It is not self-healing, self-regulating, and self-maintaining. Yet rarely does anyone ask, "Why isn't my body working right anymore?" They are just generally looking for an answer to fix it. Many times, the side effects of the solutions are worse than the problems themselves.

Let me give you an example. If someone has swollen legs, their doctor will prescribe diuretics (water pills), which will alter their kidney function to reduce the water in their blood vessels, relieving their symptoms. We still must ask ourselves, "What controls kidney function?" It is, of course, the innate intelligence being sent between your brain and kidney through the nervous system. The drugs give your nervous system a different external stressor that causes it to adapt differently and tell the kidneys to release more sodium into the urine, which helps to remove water from the blood vessels. Since the nervous system runs everything, when you interfere with nerve function, you are affecting not just one system, but all your systems. You can't just target the kidneys because you are targeting the nervous system. This is why pharmaceutical drugs have so many side effects.

When someone becomes chronically fatigued, irritable, and has mood swings, sleeping problems, weight gain, brittle nails, and thinning hair, their doctor will typically do blood work. Let's say they find that the person has low thyroid function. Their thyroid is not producing enough thyroid hormone, meaning their body is not adapting properly to its environment. So, they will typically put them on thyroid medication, which, in many cases, improves the symptoms. But since they are taking a thyroid hormone externally, the brain then believes there is plenty of thyroid hormone, causing it to produce less. Even though your symptoms improve, your thyroid becomes less healthy. Rarely do people ask "Why isn't my thyroid functioning/adapting properly?" They just want the symptoms gone.

We should be asking these questions. We should be managing our health, not our symptoms. The quality of our questions affects the quality of our health. When someone has a health crisis, we should first look at what is controlling the system that is no longer adapting properly. If we look first to find out why our bodies aren't adapting properly and look for solutions that can potentially get our bodies back to being able to self-heal, self-regulate, and self-maintain, we have a chance of keeping our health for as long as possible. When you start interfering with the system that regulates everything, it is oftentimes the beginning of the end. That is how my mom ended up on eighteen different medications, feeling anxious, depressed, and even suicidal with no hope for a future. She is not alone. Millions are living her nightmare.

It is like driving down an icy road and your car starts to slide. You correct (adapt) but end up overcorrecting slightly, requiring more correction in the other direction. You then must correct even more in the other direction. You can see where I'm going with this. This is how many people end up so unhealthy, living on multiple lifestyle drugs for blood pressure, cholesterol, osteoporosis, sleep, digestive issues, hormone issues, etc. Then they take many more for the side effects of those. Your nervous system isn't just adapting to your natural internal and external environment, it also has to find a way to adapt to the biochemical nightmare it is having to deal with. No matter where you are in your life, you need to find a way back to where your body can do the work on its own. It really begins with a belief in your own body's power to heal, adapt, self-regulate, and create homeostasis without interference from the system that controls it. Without the faith and belief in these principles, most people will feel like a victim of their circumstances, and not take action. Most people want the quick fix without a concern for the consequences. Even though living a healthy life can be simple, it takes time to change. ***CORE Principle #4: Health and healing take time and are a continuous process.***

If we know that the body is not adapting properly, then the real question is, "What can we actively do to get our bodies to function better?" We tend to take our bodies for granted until they aren't functioning properly or are breaking down. Don't wait until it's too late. Everything discussed earlier will help your body to be able to adapt at its best. Do as much as you can to provide the nutrients your body needs to be healthy. You also must avoid anything that interferes with or affects your nervous system. This includes toxins, foods, pharmaceutical drugs, poor posture, and back and neck injuries. You can avoid consuming toxins, toxic foods, and pharmaceutical drugs, but it is important that you correct poor posture and get current and past back and neck injuries corrected, as these have a direct impact on your nervous system and therefore also your health.

Many people minimize the effects of a poor diet, lack of exercise, consuming pharmaceutical drugs, poor sleeping habits, too much stress, toxic home and work environments, poor posture, and not correcting spine problems. These are all things you have some direct control over based on your choices. Remember, your nervous system runs everything so you must take care of it if you want to live a healthy, happy, and fulfilling life. You have more control than you think. Make good choices!

CHAPTER 15

Using Chiropractic Care for the Health of It

*"Medicine is the study of disease and what
causes a person to die. Chiropractic is the study
of health and what causes a person to live."*
—BJ Palmer

S o how do we take care of our spines? Our sick care system
isn't about correcting problems, it is about alleviating pain
and symptoms. Chiropractic addresses these problems for
correction. Most people think of chiropractic as something
you do for back or neck pain, but that is only the tip of
the iceberg. Chiropractic is really about analyzing the spine
for proper alignment and function and correcting it to be as
close to normal as possible for each person.

Many chiropractors practice an allopathic model of
chiropractic, where they focus on alleviating back pain. Yet,
chiropractic has so much more potential when practiced
from a corrective approach. I have witnessed it for more than
thirty years in my practice. In many cases, the very first step is
alleviating the pain, but that is just the beginning. I think it is
important to find a chiropractor that takes a more corrective

approach to correcting and maintaining a healthy spine to achieve the greatest health potential. When your spine is in proper alignment and is functioning properly, it not only feels better, but your nervous system can also function at its best. This allows the best communication from your brain to your body, which gives your body the greatest chance for maximum health potential.

Just look at these stories to show how chiropractic care can affect the body.

▎MY STORY

When I began college, I thought I wanted to study computer science. Soon after starting, I realized that I needed to find a different direction. During my second year, I injured my neck when I landed on my head while attempting a backflip in a park. For the next couple of weeks, I walked around with my head almost resting on my shoulder. I couldn't turn my head and was in significant pain with a constant headache. A friend told me that I should see his chiropractor. I made an appointment, and he took X-rays. He told me that I had a reversed curve in my neck that looked like it had been there for years, and I was already developing degeneration. As a nineteen-year-old, I was shocked I was already developing arthritis. I thought it was an old person's disease. He explained that it wasn't a disease at all; it was just mechanical wear and tear to a joint that was injured and didn't heal properly. Degeneration doesn't require being old; it just requires time. I recalled multiple traumas from early in my childhood. I had many nasty crashes from jumping ramps on my bike, playing sports, getting into multiple car accidents, and more. Oh, and also significant birth trauma. It totally made sense.

After my very first adjustment, I felt like a light came on. It was like someone just turned up the dimmer switch. Not only did it help me with my pain, but I also felt like colors were brighter, my senses were more acute, I was clearer headed, and my headache was gone. It not only helped me heal from my injury but there were also many other benefits. For years, I lived with recurring sinus infections and frequent sinus headaches. Now they were gone. It was amazing! For years I had "popped" my neck and back because it felt good. But after I got adjusted, I realized I had been "popping" my neck and back because I was almost always uncomfortable. I never felt like I was unhealthy or sick or even had any health problems. I just thought frequent headaches, sinus infections, and almost constant neck and back discomfort were normal for me. I know better now.

After that first adjustment, I had one of those aha moments. I knew right then that I was going to be a chiropractor. I thought if I could do that for other people and get paid for it, then I'm in! The rest is history. I found out what classes I need to start taking and fast-tracked through college and chiropractic college. I took accelerated classes and attended school through every summer. I wanted to start practicing as soon as I could. At the time I am writing this, I have been a chiropractor for thirty-three years. It has been an awesome journey.

Once I graduated and became a licensed chiropractor, I discovered what chiropractic really is and the impact that an adjustment can have on the human body. The chiropractic college I went to taught me a mechanistic, therapeutic approach to treating back and neck pain. I was excited to just do that. But once I started working as a chiropractor and saw firsthand the impact an adjustment had on people,

I was amazed. When I learned how and why adjusting the spine made such an impact on people's health beyond their back and neck pain, it made complete sense and resonated with my beliefs. Even after seeing it day after day, it still shocks me that the world is so unaware of the benefits. I had always believed that the body was designed to be healthy. My personal beliefs were that the closer we get to nature and allowing the body to function on its own, the better we would be. I found out that my chosen chiropractic profession had been founded on those same principles. These principles in essence stated that there is an intelligence that runs the body. This intelligence is transmitted through the nervous system from the brain to the body through a mental impulse. Distortions of alignment or function of the spine, referred to in chiropractic as subluxations, cause interference with the mental impulse and reduce your health potential and your body's ability to adapt properly to its environment. Thus, adjustments to correct subluxations in the spine not only improve the alignment and function of the spine but also reduce the interference, which improves the body's ability to express its true health potential and ability to adapt to its environment. Understanding these principles explained why so many people had, what they would consider to be, miracles happen when they got adjusted. When you understand why so many conditions improve through chiropractic care, you realize that the miracle is life itself. We take it for granted until we lose it. Chiropractic only improves function and removes interference so your body can get back to doing what it's been doing your whole life. That's the miracle!

▎SUZANNE

Suzanne had been a dental hygienist for fifteen years when she first came to see me. She came in because she was having headaches, neck pain, and upper back pain. After finding that she had spinal misalignments and vertebrae in her neck that were not functioning well, I took X-rays, including motion X-rays, of her neck. She had significant degeneration between C4–C6 and a reversed curve in her neck with the apex at those levels. I explained to her that the problems she was having in her neck were likely the cause of her headaches and neck pain and also explained where those nerves go and what systems they supply. I let her know that those nerves go down into her arms and hands, but they also control the thyroid gland.

At the end of a corrective program of care, I took post X-rays, and she had made amazing changes. Her headaches, neck pain, and upper back pain were all gone. She shared with me that she had been on thyroid medication for the past four years. She'd gone to her medical doctor because she was dealing with fatigue, sleeping problems, irritability, brittle nails, and thinning hair. After running a blood test, her doctor said she had low thyroid. She was put on thyroid medication and had been taking it for the past four years. She said the symptoms improved some, but she was still having all the problems. But after getting chiropractic adjustments, her hair started getting thicker and her nails were getting stronger, she had more energy, and she was sleeping better. She even noted that her body temperature was better regulated.

Remembering what I had said about the thyroid, she decided to do an experiment without telling her doctor or me. She started to wean herself off the thyroid medication and her symptoms continued to improve. After a couple of months of being completely off the medication, she went back to her doctor and asked to have a new blood test done. Her thyroid was working perfectly without any medication. Coincidence?

She told me that she went back to her medical doctor and told them what had happened. She told them that when I had taken the X-rays, I showed her where the damage was to the spine and explained the impact those nerves have on the control of the thyroid gland. She explained that after correcting the spinal function, the nerves were working better, and her thyroid gland started working on its own. Her doctor said that it made complete sense that if you could improve the nerve function of the thyroid, the thyroid would work better on its own.

ALICIA

I was fortunate as a young chiropractor to have many experiences that shaped my future as a chiropractor. When I had only been a chiropractor for a couple of years, I was teaching a health class and we ended up discussing childbirth and the effect it can have on the spine, especially when they used forceps or vacuum extractors. One of the women in the class broke down crying and later told me her story. Her daughter, an eighteen-year-old single mom on welfare, had a daughter named Alicia three months earlier. At one point during labor, the baby went into distress. The doctor panicked and called upstairs for a specialist. He said that the cord was wrapped around Alicia's neck. When the specialist got there, he immediately grabbed the forceps and pulled Alicia out. This grandma said she watched Alicia's tiny little neck stretch to three or four times its normal length. Alicia was rushed to the NICU and was fed through a tube in her stomach for the first six weeks of her life, was paralyzed from the neck down, and would go more than a week between bowel movements that appeared to be excruciatingly painful. Alicia had never smiled or laughed and had not made eye contact with even her mom. At some point, they sent Alicia home from the hospital, as her grandma put it, "to die."

I told her to bring her in so I could check her. The next morning, she came in with her daughter and Alicia. Alicia seemed lifeless. Normally if you lay a baby on their back, they have a flexion response. They will bring their arms and legs into a flexed position. She just laid there lifeless. Her tiny body was flaccid. She was breathing but wouldn't or couldn't make eye contact. It just seemed like nobody was home. I checked her neck, and the top bone in her neck, the atlas, was shifted to the right. It was shifted so far to the right that you could visibly see it but couldn't even feel it on the left. Knowing that this shift in alignment was likely putting pressure on the brainstem, I felt confident that I could help her. I knew it was important for me to see an X-ray first, though. When I got the X-ray, it confirmed what I had thought.

I started by just gently holding Alicia's head and applying gentle pressure to her atlas in the direction it needed to move. I knew her life was dependent on it, so I checked and adjusted her every hour the first day and four times for the next two days. There was only slight movement on the first day; however, on the second day, the atlas began to let go, and I felt something shift. On the third day, she made eye contact with her mom for the first time. On the fourth day, she had her first normal bowel movement and began going regularly after that. She started holding her head up, getting strength into her arms and legs, and breathing better. She was coming back to life. We watched every system in her body come back to life. As a young chiropractor, seeing the impact that even a very gentle adjustment can have on the entire body and how life expresses itself through the nervous system was powerful. It made sense out of everything I knew.

Alicia still had the innate intelligence that runs her body, and it was accessible. It was just being interfered with between the brain and the body. The doctors told mom and grandma that Alicia had brain damage from anoxia, or a lack of oxygen to the brain for too long, because the umbilical cord was wrapped around her neck in utero. I'm not an obstetrician, but I don't believe that Alicia was breathing through her mouth in utero. Since she is living in amniotic fluid, I'm pretty sure that she was getting oxygen through the umbilical cord from her mom. It just made more sense to me that pulling her through the birth canal by her neck was more likely the culprit.

Chiropractic doesn't treat thyroid problems, allergies, asthma, constipation, acid reflux, fatigue, sleeping problems, skin problems, or any other chronic health problems. Remember, nothing needs to be "treated." The body takes care of that. Chiropractic work removes the interferences that are preventing the body from working perfectly. So, yes, all of these problems and many more get better with chiropractic care, but chiropractic isn't treating those issues. Few people know how much chiropractic care can help. I hear the same stories from chiropractors all over the world. It still surprises me that more people aren't aware of how chiropractic works. I personally don't even see chiropractic as a treatment for back or neck pain. It is a process to get your spine and nervous system working at their best. When your spine and nervous system are working at their best, you not only don't have back or neck pain, but all the other systems work better too. I've seen almost every system in the body improve through chiropractic care, and yet we don't treat any of them. Pretty amazing! It's what I love about chiropractic!

Just like everything else in this book, chiropractic fits in a true healthcare system. Just like eating a good diet, exercising regularly, and getting good sleep, keeping a healthy spine and nervous system is a lifelong journey. If you quit taking care of your teeth, they rot. If you don't take care of your spine, it degenerates. Yes, we help people through crises if they have an injury or chronic pain or health problems. That's part of the crisis/sick care system. Dentistry and chiropractic are both part of our crisis/sick care system and also an important part of a true healthcare system. Dentistry helps people in crisis, but it is also part of a true healthcare system since the primary focus is on healthy daily practices. Someone may need a root canal, but if they don't brush and floss, they will always be needing dentistry for crisis/sick care. The same is true for chiropractic. If you don't maintain a healthy spine, you will likely need crisis care at some point. Health care is what we do through our regular routines to keep our bodies healthy.

If you give drugs or surgery to a perfectly healthy person, they only get less healthy. It only fits in a sick care model. If you give an adjustment to a spine that has improper alignment or function, moving it toward better alignment and function, whether a person has symptoms or not, they get healthier. Just like exercise and nutrition can make a healthy person healthier, chiropractic can also make healthy people healthier. Chiropractic makes the most difference when you use it for health care rather than only for crisis/sick care. Fix the problems you have, and then keep your spine healthy for a lifetime.

SECTION 4

Getting Back to Nature and Preparing our Bodies for a Healthy Life

"The wisdom of the body is responsible for 90% of the hope for patients to recover. The body has a super wisdom that is in favor of life, rather than death. This is the power that we depend on for life. All doctors are responsible for letting their patients know of this great force working within them."
—Dr. Richard Cabot, Harvard Medical School

CHAPTER 16

How Did Medicine Become Mainstream and Nature Become the Alternative?

"The goal of life is living in agreement with nature."
—Zeno

Nature got it right! It doesn't need help. It just needs no interference. After adjusting hundreds of babies and seeing the amazing results of just removing the blockage and interference to the expression of life in the body, it still surprises me that having babies checked for spinal alignment and function hasn't become a standard of care. Instead, we are making C-sections, inducing labor, and other unnecessary medical interventions standard of care. I'm not sure how we got to the place where our standards of care are a big part of our problem. If you just look at the CDC website, you'll see that we have the highest maternal and fetal mortality rates among most of the industrialized countries. It is safer to have a baby in some third-world countries than in the US.

We have great technology to save lives during childbirth; however, when you take a good thing and abuse it, the very same thing that was saving lives starts taking lives. That's what happened with antibiotics. They saved millions of lives, but then they started giving them to every man, woman, and child, whether they needed it or not. And guess what happened? Superbugs! Antibiotic resistance happened. Just like the human body is adaptable (CORE principle #5), so are viruses. It's in the definition of life. Intelligence! Adaptability! Some hospitals in Florida have a 90 percent C-section rate. There is a movement in our country to make C-sections the standard of care. Everyone will just schedule their birth. The US not only has the highest fetal and mortality rates among industrialized countries, but also the highest intervention rates in the world. Can you see the correlation? Did I mention nature got it right? How did childbirth become a medical procedure?

Skye and Jaz. My twins, Skye and Jaz, just turned seventeen this last year. When my wife Zan was pregnant with them, she wanted to have a home birth; however, due to liability issues with delivering twins at home, we couldn't find a midwife. We decided to have them at the hospital. During the numerous conversations we had with the doctor to review our birthing plan, we made it very clear that she needed to consult with me prior to using a vacuum extractor on either of them. Zan is one of the toughest people I know and was determined to have them both naturally. In the hospital, she was asked if she wanted drugs or an epidural, and she refused. I heard nurses ask why she wanted to do it naturally when she could be drugged and not have to feel it. She told them that she wanted to be present for the birth of her babies and be able to experience their birth. I was so proud of her, but they just thought she was crazy. After Skye was born, I was checking his spine and giving him his first adjustment when I looked over and the doctor had the vacuum extractor in hand ready to latch onto Jazzy's skull. We made eye contact, and she knew she had made a mistake. She put it down and tried to explain why she thought it was necessary. It became very clear that it wasn't necessary, just convenient. I feel certain she had thought that when I wasn't looking, she could get away with it to speed up the process. She said that Jaz was struggling to come out, so she was going to have to intervene. Our midwife, who was in the room but was told that she was not to talk to the doctor, whispered to me, "Ask the doctor to have Zan shift her position to create more ease for Jaz to be born." That's all it took. This experience made it clear to me that doctors are trained to deliver babies like it is a medical procedure, while others are taught to assist moms in being able to deliver their own babies. It is the system that is flawed. It is more convenient to schedule C-section deliveries to work around doctors' schedules and hospital and birthing center schedules, etc. What if we thought only about the health of moms and their babies? What would we do then? What if we did everything possible to let nature take its course and only intervened and used our amazing technology when absolutely necessary? Wow! What a concept!

This is a book about simplifying living a healthy life. How about we start in the beginning when life begins and do it right? Allow the process to happen naturally—innately—and your body will have the greatest chance for success. Thankfully, we have medical practice and intervention when things go wrong. But we use them a lot more than we need them. Making C-sections the standard of care is just wrong. We need a wake-up call! If you start down that road of medical intervention in the beginning, it just becomes a way of life. We have somehow lost faith in the potential of the human body. We must take back our power!

CHAPTER 17

Seattle to Portland Bike Ride—Preparing Your Body for a Healthy Life

"You can map out a fight plan or a life plan, but when the action starts, it may not go like you planned, and you are down to your reflexes- that means your preparation. That's where your roadwork shows. If you cheated on that in the dark of the morning, well you're going to get found out now, under the bright lights."
—Joe Frazier

I had been asked by some friends to ride in the Seattle to Portland bike ride, the STP. It was a two-hundred-mile bike ride from Seattle to Portland. I thought it sounded like fun, so I said I would love to go. They were all endurance athletes and had run triathlons and marathons. While I worked out every day, endurance wasn't my thing. They asked if I had been riding and if I felt like I could handle it. My response was simple: "How hard could it be? It's like riding a bike."

I didn't own a bike and hadn't ridden one since I was a teenager but felt that I was in good shape, so it would be no problem. I borrowed a bike from a friend, not to train, but just for the race. If you had asked me a few days before the race how I was going to prepare, I would have told you I was going to get a good night's sleep the night before, get up early, have a great breakfast, do some stretching and warm up, and drink lots of water. What actually happened was I went out the night before and had a few drinks, went to bed late, got up late, and grabbed an Egg McMuffin from McDonald's on the way to the starting line.

In the beginning, I treated it like a race and wanted to see how many bikes I could pass. Every time we came to a stoplight, bikers were backed up. So when the light turned green, I would sprint to try to get to the front of the pack. It was a fun game for me, but I didn't take it very seriously and didn't even drink much water to keep hydrated. It didn't take very long before I got a cramp in my right hamstring. So I pedaled hard, then coasted while straightening out my right leg and stretching my hamstring. About halfway to where we would end day one, my left hamstring started to cramp. So now I had to alternate which hamstring to stretch. About every half hour I got off my bike, stretched for a while, and rested. Because of this, all the people that I had passed were now passing me. I went from having to stop every half hour, to stopping every twenty minutes, to then stopping every ten minutes.

I began to feel like there was no way I could possibly make it, and just when I thought I was going to have to give up, I saw a sign, 6 MILES TO CHEHALIS. I had made it this far so nothing could stop me from making it six more miles. If I had to walk and push my bike the last couple of miles, I would. When I rounded the corner, I saw a straight road with a gradual incline that stretched all the way to the horizon.

Because of the incline I couldn't coast or stretch. Both of my quads were starting to cramp now too. I got off my bike a couple of times to rest and stretch, but I would only last about a hundred yards before cramping up again. I decided to try and push through. Suddenly, both of my hamstrings and both my quads cramped at the same time. My legs were totally seized up and in excruciating pain. I couldn't get my feet out of the toe clips. I was losing speed fast and starting to wobble. I knew I was going down. I ended up upside down in a four-foot-deep irrigation ditch with my feet stuck in the toe clips of my bike. People had to help detach me from my bike, and at that point, I couldn't even walk. Someone came and loaded me and my bike in the back of a pickup truck and hauled me and my bike to my hotel in Chehalis. I could hardly walk the next day and then had to get a ride to Portland.

I learned a valuable lesson that day. We need to prepare ourselves for the stresses that we put our bodies under. I'm sure it seems obvious that I could've had a totally different outcome for that weekend. I could've made it to Chehalis and ridden into Portland the next day. All I needed to do was train and prepare my body for that race.

This applies to all of us in our everyday lives. We tend to think we are invincible until we get sick. Too many people wander through life not living a lifestyle that prepares them for life's stresses. Then, when our health fails us, we rely on our doctors, prescription drugs, and our failed healthcare system to try to fix us. Look at how many people live an unhealthy lifestyle and then feel like a victim when they get sick or unhealthy. This also does not seem very bright. Just like in my story of the STP, where you could probably tell how it was going to end, you can watch how people live their lives and predict how it will end. If you look at our elderly, you will see too many have way too much misery, disability, and suffering. It doesn't have to be this way.

CONCLUSION

"Self-responsibility is the core quality of the fully mature,
fully functioning, self-actualizing individual."
—Brian Tracy

With so much contradictory information out there, you must do your own research and draw your own conclusions. If you choose not to and want to continue to believe that everything you hear from the pharmaceutical industry and your doctors is the truth, you might be choosing to bury your head in the sand. Most of the information your doctors are getting about prescription drugs are coming from pharmaceutical companies and reps. Even much of the research done in the medical journals, if you look closely, is funded by pharmaceutical companies or people that potentially have financial gain. It's the world we live in. It is the system that is flawed. As a culture, we have bought into it, and we are now living with the consequences of that belief system. Who should you trust? Trust your body and the innate intelligence that runs it. Choose to live a healthy life so your body will take care of you.

Until we can sit back and look at the magnitude of the problem that we have created and the global belief systems that have created it, we won't be able to change it. We must take an honest look at our reality. If we can do that, I think we have the potential to change it. The details of what we need to do are not nearly as important as it is to shift the entire paradigm. I believe that it is all about developing principles to live by. If people were solid in their principles and lived by them, they wouldn't be so terrified by the next virus and wouldn't be spending so much time in the emergency rooms and urgent care centers. Instead, they would spend more time taking care of themselves, and the food industry would have to change because people wouldn't be buying the junk they are selling. It's simple! If we have more healthy people, we will have fewer sick people.

If you develop principles to live by, then you will question anything that goes against your principles, and then make an educated decision for yourself and accept responsibility for those decisions. It's that simple!

SUMMARY

If we are going to take our power back, it all starts with our beliefs.

We must

- change our health paradigm
- develop solid principles to live by
- trust that the body is designed to be healthy, and an innate inborn intelligence runs and regulates it
- believe that if we can create a healthier body, it will take better care of us

We must do better if we want better. It's as simple as that.

▌CORE PRINCIPLES:

1. The human body is self-healing, self-regulating, and self-maintaining, and an inborn, innate intelligence runs, regulates, coordinates, and regenerates every organ and system of the body.
2. You are responsible for your life and health.
3. If you give your body more of what it needs and avoid more toxic things, you will become healthier.
4. Health and healing take time and are a continuous process.
5. The human body is adaptable.

<u>Six Steps to Creating a Healthy Lifestyle:</u>

- Become aware
- Change your attitude and belief system
- Figure out your why
- Set goals
- Commit
- Take action

<u>Eight Areas of Life to Focus On:</u>

- Diet
- Exercise
- Sleep
- Stress
- Emotional/mental health
- Relationships
- Body composition
- Healthy spine and nervous system

Since nature got it right and we have an innate intelligence that is designed to keep us healthy, it's important to create a healthy body, take good care of your spine and nervous system, and avoid things that are toxic to your body and nervous system. Develop core principles to live by, and when making choices, always ask yourself if your choices are in alignment with your principles. If you do that, you will live a healthy, happy, and empowered life.

- Take an honest look at where you are in your life
- Believe that you can change your outcome
- Decide to change
- Set goals
- Commit
- *Take action!*

WOW! It all makes sense, doesn't it? If you eat what they tell you to eat, and then when you are unhealthy, you take what they tell you to take, you will rely on a sick care system to manage your symptoms and health conditions for the rest of your life and feel like a victim of it.

-OR-

You could choose to live **the CORE Life**. You could choose to simplify healthy living and live by **CORE Principles** and accept responsibility for your life and health.

The choice is yours. *Choose wisely, my friend!* I wish you the best on your quest for the greatest life you can have. *Go for it. Take action now!* Make it happen!

Made in USA - North Chelmsford, MA
1383709_9798887598796
09.11.2023 0854